Mastering Project Management

Mastering Project Management

PMP *and Agile for Leaders*

Rupal Jain

BEP

BUSINESS EXPERT PRESS

Leader in applied, concise business books

Mastering Project Management: PMP and Agile for Leaders

Copyright © Business Expert Press, LLC, 2025

Cover design by Brent Beckley

Interior design by Exeter Premedia Services Private Ltd., Chennai, India

First published in 2024 by
Business Expert Press, LLC
222 East 46th Street, New York, NY 10017
www.businessexpertpress.com

ISBN-13: 978-1-63742-710-1 (paperback)
ISBN-13: 978-1-63742-711-8 (e-book)

Business Expert Press Portfolio and Project Management Collection

First edition: 2024

10 9 8 7 6 5 4 3 2 1

Description

In today's rapidly evolving professional landscape, *Mastering Project Management* is paramount to achieve success. This book meets the demand for a comprehensive resource that supports transferable skills, practical application, and facilitates exam readiness.

Tailored for current and aspiring project managers across various industries and disciplines, it equips readers with transferable skills applicable worldwide. Embracing a holistic approach, the book delves into essential technical and managerial processes, fostering proficiency in management and leadership skills. Moreover, it serves as a valuable guide for navigating challenging certification exams like the PMP.

The content is presented concisely, minimizing the need for frequent glossary references, and includes practical tips for addressing complex questions. Designed to facilitate efficient study, the book utilizes concise table formats and promotes SMART learning techniques. Grounded in the PMBOK Guide and enriched with Agile principles, it offers a comprehensive yet succinct exploration of crucial topics.

May this book serve as a trusted companion on your journey to professional excellence—empowering you to achieve your goals with clarity, agility, and unwavering determination.

Keywords

project management; PMP exam preparation; PMP certification; agile; PMBOK guide; manager; project management professional; exam success tips; leadership; easy PMP

Contents

List of Figures

List of Tables

From the Author's Desk

Today's demanding environment requires laser-sharp focus and efficient learning. With project management playing a pivotal role in dynamic business environments, there is a pressing need for a resource that combines comprehensive guidance, catering to a broad audience-seeking success in project management roles. Despite my best efforts with existing resources, I found countless study materials lacking the conciseness and effectiveness needed to truly excel in certification exams such as Project Management Professional (PMP). This gap inspired me to write this book. My book is uniquely crafted to serve dual purposes: it not only provides effective preparation for exams like the PMP but also equips readers with the concepts essential for becoming an excellent project manager.

Geared toward both current and aspiring project managers, this book imparts transferable skills applicable across diverse industries such as Semiconductor, Engineering, IT, Construction, and global contexts.

I have emphasized a holistic perspective to guide readers through technical and managerial processes for the path toward becoming a successful PMP. It prioritizes key information, ensuring that definitions and synonyms for critical terms are presented alongside the text, eliminating the need for frequent glossary references. Key tips and quick bites are helpful to crack mindset and scenario-based complex questions. The book is designed to facilitate SMART and efficient study methods through concise table formats, promoting simultaneous learning and exam success.

With the intent to position this book as offering unique project management content aligned with PMI process areas, I am confident that this study guide, coupled with dedicated time for mock tests and exam environment simulation, is sufficient for anyone to pass the PMP exam on their first attempt.

Rooted in "A Guide to the Project Management Body of Knowledge (PMBOK Guide), all rights reserved by PMI"—the book encapsulates essential topics, providing Balanced depth and brevity. By integrating PMP and Agile principles, the book equips readers with a comprehensive skill set that is relevant and adaptable to modern project management practices.

The production process of this book has involved several critical stages, including writing, peer reviews, proofreading, and incorporating feedback, all within a comprehensive quality management system. I have diligently endeavored to ensure the book is free from errors to the best of my ability. However, should any mistakes have inadvertently occurred, I sincerely regret them and would be immensely grateful to anyone who brings them to my attention. Please note that we do not assume legal responsibility, and the author shall not be liable for any direct, indirect, incidental, consequential, or punitive damages arising from the use of or inability to use the content of this book.

May you all be blessed with success!!
Rupal Jain
Author
Mastering Project Management: PMP and Agile for Leaders

Acknowledgments

Bringing this book to life wouldn't have been possible without the dedication of many individuals.

I would like to express my sincere thanks to the amazing team at Business Express Press. Their expertise, guidance, and support throughout the publishing process were invaluable. Special thanks to Scott Isenberg, Kam Jugdev, Jim Spohrer, and Charlene Kronstedt for their contributions at various stages. Your hard work and dedication are deeply appreciated.

Of course, I wouldn't be here without the unwavering support of the almighty and my loving family members. To my husband, Rajat, I owe a debt of gratitude for his immense support throughout this journey.

Thank you all for believing in me and this book.

I wish you all the best!
Rupal Jain

CHAPTER 1

Introduction to PMP Exam

The Project Management Professional (PMP) certification is a globally recognized credential for individuals in the field of project management for various industries. Offered by the Project Management Institute (PMI), it signifies expertise in leading and directing projects.

Here's a guide on how to ace the PMP certification.

Eligibility Criteria

- Ensure you meet the eligibility requirements, which typically include a four-year degree, 36 months of project management experience, and 35 hours of project management education. Refer to the PMI website to get the latest information on eligibility criteria.
- Once your application is submitted, you have approximately a year to take the exam. Note that the applications can be audited randomly.

Understand the Exam Format

- Familiarize yourself with the PMP Exam Content Outline provided by PMI.[19] Understand the domains, tasks, and skills required for the exam. I have briefed on this in the upcoming chapters.
- The exam consists of 180 questions, out of which 175 are marked. You have 230 minutes in total to answer 180 questions. The questions are split into three sets of 60 questions each. After every set (60 questions), you may take a 10-minute scheduled break. These 10-minute breaks are exclusive of the 230 minutes, and you might not be

allowed to exit the building during this time. You can take an unscheduled break anytime during the examination, but those will be counted from 230 minutes (so be careful in choosing that unless it is extremely urgent).

Understand the Exam Outline

The exam is structured around five domains, each representing a specific area of project management. The current domains and their approximate percentage weightings are as follows:[10]

- People (42 percent): Emphasizes the skills and activities associated with effectively leading a project team.
- Process (50 percent): Focuses on the processes and activities involved in planning and managing a project, including the Project Life Cycle.
- Business Environment (8 percent): Addresses the broader organizational context in which projects operate, considering factors such as organizational culture and structure.

Please note that these percentages are approximate and may be subject to change. PMI periodically updates the Exam Content Outline, and it's essential to refer to the most recent version provided by PMI for the latest information on their website.

There is no officially defined percentage required to pass the exam, but the marking is designated NI (Needs Improvement), BT (Below Target), T (Target), and AT (Above Target). Scoring a minimum average of T combined from all sections should be good.

Mode of Exam

- You have the feasibility to take an exam from a Pearson[19] VUE venue/test center OR online. There are pros and cons for both modes.

- Pearson VUE Test Center: The exam is still online and taken on a computer. But you would not have to worry about Internet speed. The exam room is monitored by audio and video.
- Home-Based Online Exam: Ensure your computer/system has a good Internet connection. You can perform a speed test through Pearson VUE (for more details, refer to the website on how to set it up and what the other requirements are).
- PROS: Comfort of home (nothing can beat that).
- CONS: Be careful with the system settings and leaving your exam space. There are strict rules, permissions required you might want to check (refer to Pearson VUE website). The exam is monitored via audio and video through a webcam.

Study Resources

- PMP[19] is one of the most challenging examinations and having good study resources is essential. There are ample lengthy resources available in the market which can make aspirants tired and lost, so streamlining your study with important topics for examination is needed, other than understanding the essence of project management.
- This book streamlines the path to certification as it includes topics important for the examination, drawing on my own as well as many others' experiences to provide laser-focused insights.
- To draw the best from the book, one must focus on the keywords being highlighted. They can build up good references for scenarios and help in focused preparation.
- This book will help you understand the question format and tricky keywords and answer the questions in an easier and faster way, all leading toward the path for your guaranteed success as a Project Management Professional.

Understand PMI's Perspective

- Familiarize yourself with PMI's approach to project management using PMBOK (the official guide to project management). Understand their terminology and how they expect project managers[1] to handle various scenarios. Don't worry, this book will get you there.

Stay Confident

- Trust your preparation and enter the exam with confidence. Manage your time effectively during the exam, and don't dwell too long on challenging questions. Flag the questions you are unsure about and revisit them.

  Note: **The details mentioned above may be subject to change depending on PMI. Refer to the PMI website[19] to get the latest information.**

  Remember, success in the PMP exam requires a combination of **theoretical knowledge and practical application.** Dedicate ample time to preparation and approach the exam with a strategic mindset. Good luck!

CHAPTER 2

Introduction to Project Management Processes

Project management has five crucial phases or processes: Initiating, Planning, Executing, Monitoring and Control, and Closing. It's important to understand each process's sequence, inputs, outputs, and tools when preparing for any project.

Exam tip: You don't have to memorize them but should be analytical to understand what comes after which process, and if you have been asked what project management tool you would use with a concerned process,[9] you should be able to answer.

Figure 2.1 presents a rough estimation of the project management process.

What can you infer from the Graph below?

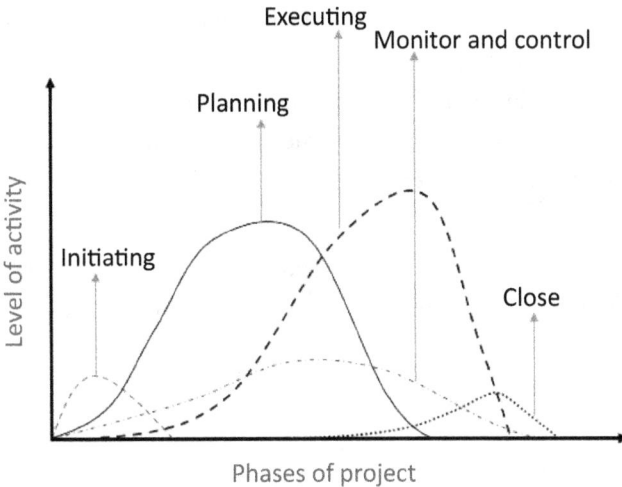

Figure 2.1 Project process groups

1. The sequence typically involves initiation, followed by planning, executing, monitoring and controlling, and finally closing. *Example*: The software development project typically starts with the **Initiation Phase**, during which project objectives are defined. This is followed by the **Planning Phase**, where tasks, timelines, and resources are allocated. Next comes the **Executing Phase**, where coding and development activities take place. The **Monitoring and Controlling Phase** is then implemented to track progress and manage any deviations from the plan. Lastly, the project is concluded with the **Closing Phase**, where the completed product is delivered and project documentation is finalized.

2. The level of activity varies depending on the project type, with certain activities potentially necessitating longer durations. For instance, projects with regulatory requirements may demand extended planning phases due to external dependencies and associated risks.

3. The period of activity fluctuates throughout the project phases. Monitoring and control activities span the entirety of the project phases. Execution typically commences after the planning stage has begun, and planning initiates only after the initiation phase has commenced. *Example*: In the development of a new product, the monitoring and control activities occur from the initial concept stage all the way through to the product launch and post-launch evaluation. Execution of the product development tasks begins once the planning phase, including market research and prototyping, is underway, which in turn commences after the initiation phase, where the project is officially approved and resources are allocated.

Table 2.1 presents the 10 knowledge areas mapped to five processes based on the PMBOK-Sixth edition.[9]

Table 2.1 Project process flow

Process Areas

Knowledge Areas

	Initiating	Planning	Executing	Monitor and Control	Close
Integration Management	1) Develop Project Charter	1) Develop Project Management Plan	1) Direct and manage project work	1) Monitor and control Project Work 2) Perform Integrated Change control	1) Close Project or phase
Scope Management		1) Plan scope management 2) Collect Requirements 3) Define Scope 4) Create WBS		1) Verify Scope 2) Control scope	
Schedule Management		1) Plan Schedule management 2) Define activities 3) Sequence activities 4) Estimate activity Durations 5) Develop Schedule		1) Control Schedule	
Cost Management		1) Plan cost management 2) Estimate costs 3) Determine Budget		1) Control Costs	
Quality Management		1) Plan Quality	1) Perform Quality assurance	1) Perform Quality control	

(Continued)

Table 2.1 (Continued)

Process Areas

Knowledge Areas	Initiating	Planning	Executing	Monitor and Control	Close
Resource Management		1) Develop Resource management plan 2) Estimate activity resources	1) Acquire Project team 2) Develop Project team 3) Manage project team		
Communication Management	1) Identify Stakeholders	1) Plan communication Management	1) Distribute Information 2) Manage stakeholders expectations	1) Report performance	
Risk Management		1) Plan risk management 2) Identify risk 3) Perform qualitative risk 4) Perform quantitative risk 5) Plan risk responses	1) Monitor and control risks		
Procurement Management		1) Plan procurement management	1) Conduct Procurements	1) Administer/control procurements	1) Close procurement management
Stakeholder Management		1) Plan stakeholder engagement	1) Manage stakeholder engagement	1) Monitor stakeholder engagement	

2.1 Stage 1—Initiating

In the **Initiating Phase**, Project Manager[1] should identify the business problem. Business cases can be used to investigate options and draft the Project Charter. It's an important stage as it *could** create a domino effect disrupting its following stages if something went wrong. Of course, there is nothing in the world that can't be fixed, and you can still come back to the problem when root cause analysis is done and define a Corrective/Preventive action through PDCA (Plan Do Check Act).

*Watch for keywords like could, may, and might (in future tense) means there is a possibility of risk. With risk comes management, risk register, risk plan, quantitative, qualitative risk analysis, and so on, which will be discussed in sections ahead.

Did you know an "Issue" is different from "Risk"?

Keywords such as "will," "certain that something will happen," and "is going to happen" often indicate a level of certainty or predictability, suggesting the presence of an issue. With issues, the need for an issue log and issue register becomes apparent. On the other hand, when discussing risks, the focus is on potential future possibilities (could, may, might).

2.1.1 Input, Output, Tools, and Techniques

Table 2.1 presents the two knowledge areas associated with "Initiating". Refer to Figure 2.2 to understand the inputs, outputs, and tools associated with them.[9]

Tip: You can effectively discern the correct response by carefully noting the keywords in multiple-choice questions (MCQs). Utilizing the method of elimination becomes essential to differentiate between options and ensure the selection of the most accurate answer, as, without attention to these keywords, all MCQs might appear similar.

The definitions below are fundamental to understanding ITTOs in project management.[9]

1. **Project:** A project refers to a **temporary** endeavor taken up to produce a distinctive product, service, or outcome. *Example*: Building a new website for a company, organizing a charity event, or implementing a new software system are all examples of projects.[1]

2. **Project Charter:** This is a formal **high-level** document issued by a **project sponsor** that authorizes the initiation of a project and grants the project manager the authority to utilize organizational resources for project activities. The Project Charter typically includes general information such as the project title, a brief description, the project manager's name, the sponsor's name, project objectives, assumptions, preliminary scope, milestones, impact statements, stakeholder details, resource requirements, success criteria, and signatures of stakeholders with signoff dates. *Example*: A project charter for a construction project may include details such as the project's purpose (e.g., building a new office complex), project manager's name, stakeholders involved, key milestones (e.g., groundbreaking ceremony, completion of the structural framework), and budget allocation.

3. **Project Management Plan:** This document integrates the various subsidiary plans of a project and establishes management controls and an overall plan for coordinating and managing the project's individual components. *Example*: A project management plan for a marketing campaign could include sections on scope management, schedule management, cost management, risk management, communication management, and quality management, outlining specific strategies and procedures for each area.[1]

4. **Stakeholder:** A stakeholder is a person, group, or organization that has the potential to impact, be impacted by, or perceive themselves as being affected by the decisions, actions, or results of a project, program, or portfolio. *Example*: In the development of a new product, stakeholders might include customers, investors, suppliers, marketing teams, and regulatory authorities, all of whom have an interest in the product's success.

5. **Stakeholder Engagement Plan:** This component of the project or program management plan outlines the strategies and actions necessary to facilitate the productive involvement of stakeholders in project or program decision making and execution. *Example*: A stakeholder engagement plan for a community development project may include regular meetings with residents, workshops to gather feedback, and newsletters to keep the community informed about project progress.

6. **Sponsor:** The sponsor, whether an individual or a group, holds the responsibility of providing resources and support to ensure the success of the project, program, or portfolio. They are held accountable for enabling its accomplishments. Note: In predictive/hybrid/waterfall, resources are usually provided by sponsor, but in agile methodology, a functional manager can be asked for the same. *Example*: In a corporate setting, the CEO or a senior executive might serve as the sponsor for a strategic initiative, providing funding, advocating for the project, and removing obstacles to its success.[1]

7. **Enterprise Environmental Factors (EEFs):** These are external conditions that influence, constrain, or direct the project, program, or portfolio and are not under the immediate control of the project team. *Example*: Market conditions, government regulations, industry standards, economic trends, and technological advancements are all examples of enterprise environmental factors that can impact a project's execution and outcomes.[21]

8. **Organizational Process Assets:** These are the plans, processes, policies, procedures, and knowledge bases specific to and utilized by the performing organization. *Example*: Organizational process assets may include templates for project documentation, historical data from past projects, lessons learned repositories, and standard operating procedures for project management activities.

9. **Product Life Cycle:** The product life cycle represents the stages of the evolution of a product from its conceptualization through delivery, growth, maturity, and eventual retirement. *Example*: The product life cycle of a smartphone includes stages such as product design, manufacturing, marketing and sales, customer usage, and eventual product discontinuation or replacement.

10. **Business Case:** This document is typically prepared prior to project planning and justifies why the project is being undertaken. It includes considering alternative options, anticipated benefits, high-level risks, costs, schedules, and a cost/benefit analysis. *Example:* A business case for implementing a new customer relationship management (CRM) system might outline the benefits of improved customer data management, increased sales productivity, and better customer service, along with the costs and potential risks associated with the project.

I. Initiating

I.1 Integration Management

Develop Project Charter

1) INPUTS: Business case, Agreements/ contracts, EEF (Enterprise Environmental Factors), OPA(Organizational Process Assets)

2) Tools and Techniques: Expert Judgment, Data gathering, Interpersonal skills, Meetings

3) OUTPUTS: Project Charter, Assumption Logs

1.2 Communication management

Identify Stakeholders

1) INPUTS: Project Charter, Business Documents, Project Management Plan, Project Documents, Agreements and contracts, EEFs, OPAs

2) Tools and Techniques: Expert Judgment. Data gathering, Data analysis, Data Representation, Meetings

3) OUTPUTS: Stakeholder register, Change requests, Project management plan updates, Project document updates

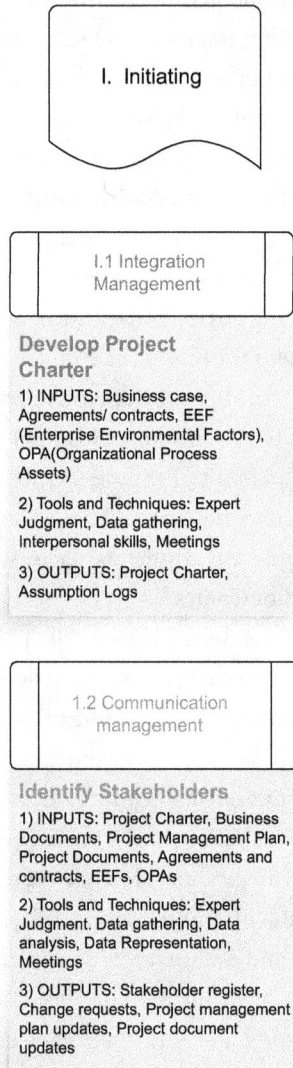

Figure 2.2 ITTO—Project lifecycle: Initiating[9]

2.1.2 Project versus Program versus Portfolio versus Operations

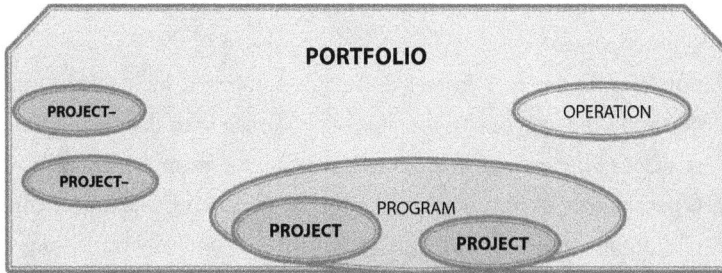

Figure 2.3 Project, Program, Operation, Portfolio

1. **Program:** An amalgamation of interconnected projects, subsidiary programs, and program activities orchestrated in a harmonized manner to attain synergistic benefits that cannot be achieved through individual management.

2. **Program Management:** The proficient application of knowledge, expertise, and principles to a program, aimed at realizing program objectives and garnering benefits and oversight that are unattainable when managing program components in isolation.

3. **Program Management Office (PMO):** A structured management framework that standardizes governance processes related to programs, facilitating the exchange of resources, methodologies, tools, and techniques.

4. **Project Steering Group Committee (PSG):** An advisory body entrusted with assisting project teams in defining directions, objectives, budgets, and timelines.[1]

5. **Program Manager:** The designated individual within the performing organization tasked with leading the team or teams responsible for achieving program objectives.[1]

6. **Phase Gate:** A comprehensive evaluation conducted at the conclusion of a phase, determining whether to proceed to the subsequent phase, continue with adjustments, or terminate a project or program.

7. **Portfolio:** A collective assembly of projects, programs, subsidiary portfolios, and operations managed as an integrated unit to realize strategic objectives.

8. **Portfolio Balancing:** The strategic process of optimizing the composition of portfolio elements to advance the organization's strategic goals effectively.

9. **Portfolio Charter:** A formal document authorized by a sponsor that delineates the structure of the portfolio, aligns it with the organization's strategic goals, and specifies the authorization for its implementation.

10. **Operations:** A continual and enduring endeavor, whereupon completion of a project's "Closure," responsibility typically transitions to the operations team through seamless hand-offs.

Examples

- **Program:** A government initiative to improve transportation infrastructure involving multiple construction projects such as road expansions, bridge repairs, and public transit enhancements.

- **Program Management:** The strategic coordination of various educational initiatives within a school district to improve student performance and teacher training.

- **Program Management Office (PMO):** A centralized department within a multinational corporation that provides standardized project management methodologies, tools, and support across all business units.

- **Project STEERING Group Committee (PSG):** An advisory committee comprising senior executives and project managers guiding a company's expansion into new markets.

- **Phase Gate:** A software development project undergoing a phase gate review before moving from the design phase to the development phase.

- **Portfolio:** A real estate investment company managing a portfolio of properties, including residential apartments, commercial buildings, and retail spaces.

- **Portfolio Balancing:** Adjusting investments across various sectors within a financial portfolio to minimize risk and maximize returns.

- **Portfolio Charter:** A document outlining the objectives and structure of a company's investment portfolio, aligning with its long-term strategic goals.

2.1.3 Types of Managers

Questions in the exam can be framed in a way where understanding differences between managers can be crucial.

Project Manager,[1] Program Manager, PMO, Functional Manager, Project Coordinator, Product Owner, and Product Manager are some of them. We have discussed some of the terms in **2.1.1.**

Business Analysts/Product Managers work with Clients to get customer requirements. Once requirements are gathered, they work with Functional Managers/Product Owners to establish those requirements. The project may be hybrid, and the agile part of that can be handled by the Product Manager and team, where there can be dotted/solid line reporting between the Product Manager[1] and Project Manager (depending on the type of organizations discussed in **2.1.3**).

Functional Managers and their teams are based on the type of skills they are efficient at. In **Agile, teams are self-organizing,** and the Project Manager **wouldn't** assign work to a team based on skills unless in a predictive style, where teams can be formed and work can be distributed based on skills by PM.

Project Coordinators are usually assistants to a Project Manager. All these positions have one thing in common. They need organizing skills with respect to people management, time management, leadership skills, along with domain experiences and knowledge.

2.1.4 Types of Organizations

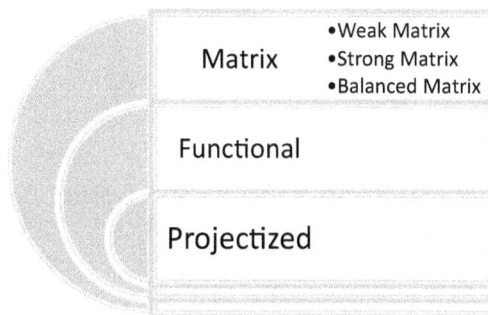

Matrix	•Weak Matrix •Strong Matrix •Balanced Matrix
Functional	
Projectized	

Figure 2.4 Types of organizations

Let's say Person A is Project manager   Person B is Functional Manager

Weak Matrix Org

Balanced Matrix Org

Strong Matrix Org

Figure 2.5 *Types of organizational influences on project: Matrix Organization*

In a Weak Matrix organization, the Project manager's authority may be limited. The Functional Manager usually controls the project budget. The Project Manager's role along with the PM staff's role can be part-time. Whereas in a Strong Matrix organization, things are just the opposite. The Project Manager's Authority is Moderate to High. The PM controls the Project Budget as well as resource availability. PM, PM Staff roles are fulltime. In a Balanced Matrix Organization, things are balanced between the Functional Manager and Project Manager.

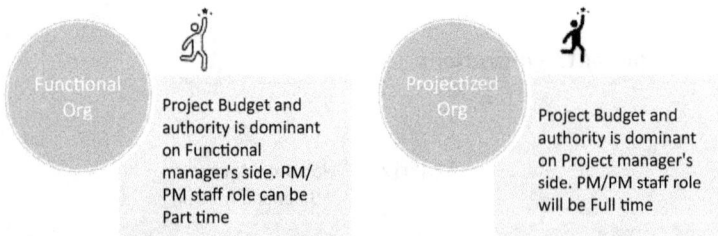

Functional Org — Project Budget and authority is dominant on Functional manager's side. PM/PM staff role can be Part time

Projectized Org — Project Budget and authority is dominant on Project manager's side. PM/PM staff role will be Full time

Figure 2.6 *Types of organizational influences on project: Functional and Projectized Organization*

2.1.5 Question and Answer Based on "Stage—Initiating"

1. **Scenario 1: Project Identification**
   - You've identified a potential project that aligns with organizational goals. What should be your next step in the initiating phase?
     a. Develop a detailed project schedule.
     b. Create a project charter. c. Assign tasks to team members.
     d. Start procurement processes.

2. **Scenario 2: Stakeholder Identification**
   - During project initiation, you discover a key stakeholder who was not initially identified. What should you do?
     a. Ignore the stakeholder to avoid complications. b. Update the stakeholder register. c. Wait until the planning phase to address the stakeholder. d. Proceed without involving the new stakeholder.

3. **Scenario 3: Project Scope Definition**
   - You are initiating a project, and the team members have different understandings of the project scope. How would you address this situation?
     a. Finalize the scope without team input. b. Conduct a scope definition workshop. c. Proceed with the majority's understanding. d. Escalate the issue to senior management.

4. **Scenario 4: Project Constraints**
   - Your project has identified several constraints, including budget limitations and a tight timeline. What is the appropriate action during project initiation?
     a. Adjust project goals to fit the constraints. b. Include constraints in the project charter. c. Ignore constraints until the planning phase. d. Seek additional funding without informing stakeholders.

5. **Scenario 5: Risk Identification**
   - While initiating a project, you identify potential risks that could impact project success. What should be your next step?
     a. Document risks and address them during execution.
     b. Develop a risk management plan. c. Ignore risks at this stage. d. Share risks with stakeholders without analysis.

6. **Scenario 6: Legal Compliance**
   - Your project involves activities subject to regulatory requirements. How should you address legal compliance during project initiation?
     a. Ignore compliance until the execution phase.
     b. Collaborate with legal experts to ensure compliance.
     c. Delegate compliance tasks to team members. d. Proceed without considering legal implications.

7. **Scenario 7: Project Approval**
   - Your project requires approval from senior management to proceed. What is a crucial document needed during project initiation to seek approval?
     a. Detailed project schedule b. Project business case
     c. Stakeholder analysis d. Team roles and responsibilities

8. **Scenario 8: Resource Identification**
   - In the initiating phase, you need to identify the resources required for the project. What is the key output of this process?
     a. Risk register b. Resource calendar c. Stakeholder register
     d. Project charter.

9. **Scenario 9: Project Sponsor**
   - During project initiation, you realize the importance of having a project sponsor. What role does the sponsor play in this phase?
     a. Develop detailed project plans. b. Provide project funding and support. c. Execute project tasks. d. Review project deliverables.

10. **Scenario 10: Project Objectives**
    - You are initiating a project and need to define clear and measurable project objectives. What is the purpose of having well-defined objectives?
      a. Attract more team members. b. Communicate project purpose and direction. c. Minimize stakeholder involvement. d. Simplify project reporting.

11. **Scenario 11: Project Assumptions**
    - You are listing project assumptions during initiation. What is the importance of documenting assumptions?
      a. Create unnecessary project constraints. b. Enhance team

collaboration. c. Provide a basis for project decision-making.
d. Increase project complexity.

12. **Scenario 12: Project Kickoff Meeting**
   - You are preparing for a project kickoff meeting during initiation. What is the primary objective of this meeting?
     a. Detailed project planning b. Introduce the project to stakeholders and team members. c. Review project progress. d. Assign tasks to team members.

13. **Scenario 13: Project Dependencies**
   - While initiating the project, you identify several dependencies between tasks. How should you manage these dependencies?
     a. Ignore dependencies until execution. b. Document dependencies and incorporate them into project plans. c. Delegate dependency management to team members. d. Address dependencies only if they become critical.

14. **Scenario 14: Stakeholder Engagement**
   - You are initiating a project and want to engage stakeholders effectively. What is a suitable approach for stakeholder engagement?
     a. Minimize stakeholder communication to avoid interference. b. Involve stakeholders in project decision-making. c. Provide stakeholders with limited project information. d. Address stakeholder concerns only during project execution.

15. **Scenario 15: Project Initiation Documents**
   - As a Project Manager, you are responsible for compiling project initiation documents. What is a key document included in this compilation?
     a. Detailed project schedule b. Project charter c. Stakeholder analysis d. Risk management plan

16. **Scenario 16: Project Feasibility**
   - You are initiating a project and want to ensure its feasibility. What aspects should you consider determining project feasibility?
     a. Stakeholder preferences only b. Budget constraints only c. Technical, financial, and organizational aspects d. Project schedule constraints only

17. **Scenario 17: Conflict Resolution**
    - During project initiation, team members have conflicting opinions on the project scope. How would you address this conflict?
    a. Ignore conflicts until they escalate. b. Collaboratively resolve conflicts with the team. c. Escalate conflicts to senior management. d. Exclude conflicting team members from the project.

18. **Scenario 18: Project Authorization**
    - You've completed the project initiation phase and need formal approval to proceed. What document is typically issued to authorize project execution?
    a. Detailed project schedule b. Project charter c. Risk management plan d. Resource calendar

19. **Scenario 19: Project Communication**
    - During initiation, you identify the need for effective project communication. What should you consider when planning project communication?
    a. Limit communication to major milestones.
    b. Communicate only with the project team. c. Tailor communication to stakeholder needs. d. Delay communication until project execution.

20. **Scenario 20: Project Closure Criteria**
    - While initiating a project, you realize the importance of establishing criteria for project closure. What is a critical factor when defining closure criteria?
    a. Ignoring stakeholder feedback b. Relying solely on budget constraints c. Aligning with project objectives and requirements d. Waiting until project execution to define closure criteria.

Answers

1. **Answer: b. Create a project charter**
    - During project initiation, creating a project charter is a crucial step to authorize the project officially.
2. **Answer: b. Update the stakeholder register**
    - Identifying new stakeholders during the project initiation phase requires updating the stakeholder register.

3. **Answer: b. Conduct a scope definition workshop**
   - To align the team's understanding of the project scope, conducting a workshop ensures clarity and consensus.
4. **Answer: b. Include constraints in the project charter**
   - Constraints, including budget and timeline, should be documented in the project charter during initiation.
5. **Answer: b. Develop a risk management plan**
   - Identifying risks during initiation necessitates the development of a comprehensive risk management plan.
6. **Answer: b. Collaborate with legal experts to ensure compliance**
   - Legal compliance is critical during initiation, and collaboration with legal experts helps ensure adherence to regulations.
7. **Answer: b. Project business case**
   - A project business case is a crucial document during initiation, presenting the justification for the project to gain approval.
8. **Answer: b. Resource calendar**
   - Identifying resources during initiation contributes to creating a resource calendar, outlining resource availability.
9. **Answer: b. Provide project funding and support**
   - The project sponsor plays a vital role during initiation by providing funding and support to initiate the project successfully.
10. **Answer: b. Communicate project purpose and direction**
    - Well-defined project objectives communicated during initiation help provide direction and purpose for the project.
11. **Answer: c. Provide a basis for project decision making**
    - Documenting assumptions during initiation provides a foundation for making informed project decisions.
12. **Answer: b. Introduce the project to stakeholders and team members**
    - The primary objective of a project kickoff meeting during initiation is to introduce the project to stakeholders and the team.

13. **Answer: b. Document dependencies and incorporate them into project plans**
    - Managing dependencies during initiation involves documenting them and considering them in project planning.
14. **Answer: b. Involve stakeholders in project decision making**
    - Effective stakeholder engagement during initiation involves involving them in project decision-making processes.
15. **Answer: b. Project charter**
    - Project initiation documents include the project charter, a key document that authorizes the project.
16. **Answer: c. Technical, financial, and organizational aspects**
    - Determining project feasibility during initiation involves considering technical, financial, and organizational aspects.
17. **Answer: b. Collaboratively resolve conflicts with the team**
    - Addressing conflicts among team members during initiation is best handled collaboratively for a positive team environment.
18. **Answer: b. Project charter**
    - Formal approval for project execution is often granted through the issuance of a project charter during initiation.
19. **Answer: c. Tailor communication to stakeholder needs**
    - Effective communication planning during initiation involves tailoring messages to meet the specific needs of stakeholders.
20. **Answer: c. Aligning with project objectives and requirements**
    - Defining closure criteria during initiation involves aligning them with project objectives and requirements for a successful conclusion.

2.2 Stage 2—Planning

These processes help to plan scope, refine objectives, and define a course of action before the next stage, "executing the project." It comprises planning ten knowledge areas.

Tip: I would suggest keeping Table 2.1 on the side while reading, so that it becomes easier for mapping.

1. Plan Integration
2. Plan Scope
3. Plan Schedule
4. Plan Cost
5. Plan Quality
6. Plan Resources
7. Plan Communication
8. Plan Risk
9. Plan Procurement
10. Plan Stakeholder

2.2.1 Plan Integration

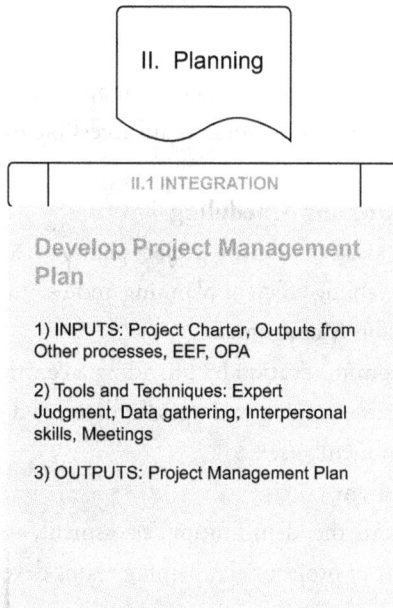

Figure 2.7 ITTO—Project lifecycle: Planning Integration[9]

2.2.1.1 PMIS

PMIS stands for Project Management Information System. It refers to a set of tools, processes, and methodologies that facilitate the collection, storage, and management of project-related information. PMIS is an essential component in project management, helping teams efficiently plan, execute, monitor, and control projects. Here are the key aspects of PMIS:

1. **Data Collection and Storage**
   - PMIS collects and stores data related to project scope, schedule, budget, resources, risks, and other relevant information.
2. **Collaboration**
   - It provides a platform for collaboration, allowing team members to share information, communicate, and work together effectively.
3. **Document Management**
   - PMIS helps manage project documentation, ensuring that the latest versions of documents are accessible to team members.
4. **Project Planning and Scheduling**
   - PMIS tools assist in creating project plans, schedules, and timelines, enabling efficient planning and resource allocation.
5. **Communication Management**
   - Facilitates communication by providing a centralized platform for exchanging messages, updates, and notifications among team members.
6. **Risk Management**
   - PMIS supports the identification, assessment, and management of project risks, helping teams develop strategies to address uncertainties.
7. **Monitoring and Reporting**
   - It enables real-time monitoring of project progress and generates reports to keep stakeholders informed about the project's status.

8. **Resource Management**
   - PMIS helps allocate and manage resources efficiently, ensuring that the right resources are available at the right time.

9. **Integration with Other Systems**
   - PMIS may integrate with other enterprise systems (e.g., finance, HR) to ensure consistency and accuracy of data across the organization.

10. **Decision Support**
   - Provides tools and analytics to support decision-making processes by offering insights into project performance and trends.

Common examples of PMIS tools include project management software, collaboration platforms, document management systems, and communication tools. The selection of PMIS depends on the specific needs and complexity of the project, as well as the preferences of the project management team.

2.2.2 Plan Scope

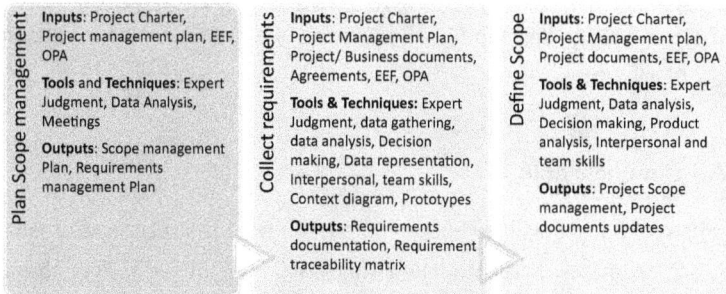

Plan Scope management	Collect requirements	Define Scope
Inputs: Project Charter, Project management plan, EEF, OPA **Tools** and **Techniques:** Expert Judgment, Data Analysis, Meetings **Outputs:** Scope management Plan, Requirements management Plan	**Inputs:** Project Charter, Project Management Plan, Project/ Business documents, Agreements, EEF, OPA **Tools & Techniques:** Expert Judgment, data gathering, data analysis, Decision making, Data representation, Interpersonal, team skills, Context diagram, Prototypes **Outputs:** Requirements documentation, Requirement traceability matrix	**Inputs:** Project Charter, Project Management plan, Project documents, EEF, OPA **Tools & Techniques:** Expert Judgment, Data analysis, Decision making, Product analysis, Interpersonal and team skills **Outputs:** Project Scope management, Project documents updates

Figure 2.8 ITTO—Project lifecycle: Planning Scope[9]

1. **Requirements Traceability Matrix:** A structured grid that establishes a clear link between product requirements and the deliverables intended to fulfill them. *Example:* A grid may link the requirement

"website login feature" to the deliverable "user authentication system."

2. **Requirements Management Plan:** A vital segment of the project or program management plan outlining the methods for analyzing, documenting, and overseeing requirements throughout the project lifecycle.

3. **Scope Baseline:** The officially approved version of a scope statement, work breakdown structure (WBS), and associated WBS dictionary. It serves as the reference point for comparing actual project outcomes and can only be altered through formal change control procedures.

4. **Scope Creep:** The unauthorized and unregulated product or project scope expansion without corresponding adjustments to project timelines, budgets, and resource allocations. *Example:* during a website redesign project, adding new features like a blog and online store in the last-minute ask, how would a project management professional work without adjusting the project timeline or budget? Refer to Fast tracking, resource optimization, and resource leveling in later sections.

5. **Scope Management Plan:** An essential component of the project or program management plan detailing the strategies and procedures for defining, developing, monitoring, controlling, and validating project scope.

2.2.3 Plan Schedule

In this section, we will be hearing about some terms such as estimates, types of estimates, Path modeling such as CPM, PERT, Gantt charts, dependency determination, leads and lags, and so on. These are important for the PMP exam.

Let's start with ITTOs for the Plan Schedule phase.

Define Activities

- Inputs: Project management plan, EEF, OPA
- Tools & Techniques: Expert Judgement, Decomposition, Rolling Wave Planning , Meetings
- Outputs: Activity list, Activity attributes, milestone list, change requests, project management plan updates

Estimate Activity durations

- Inputs: Project management Plan, Project documents, EEF, OPA
- Tools and techniques: Expert Judgement, Analogous estimating, Parametric estimating, Three point estimating, Bottom up estimating, Data analysis , Decision making, Meetings
- Outputs: Duration estimates, basis of estimates , Project document updates

Sequence activities

- Inputs: Project Management plan, Project documents, EEF, OPA
- Tools and techniques: Precedence diagramming method, Dependency determination and integration, Leads and Lags, PMIS (Project management Information System)
- Outputs: Project Schedule Network diagrams, Project document updates

Develop schedule

- Inputs: Project management plan, Project documents, Agreements, EEF, OPA
- Tools and Techniques: Schedule network analysis, Critical Path method, Resource optimization, Data analysis, Leads and Lags, schedule compression, PMIS, Agile release planning
- Outputs: Schedule baseline, Project Schedule, schedule data, Project calendars, change requests, project management plan updates, project document updates

Plan schedule management

- Inputs: Project Charter, Project management plan, EEF, OPA
- Tools and Techniques: Expert Judgement, data analysis, meetings
- Outputs: Schedule management Plan

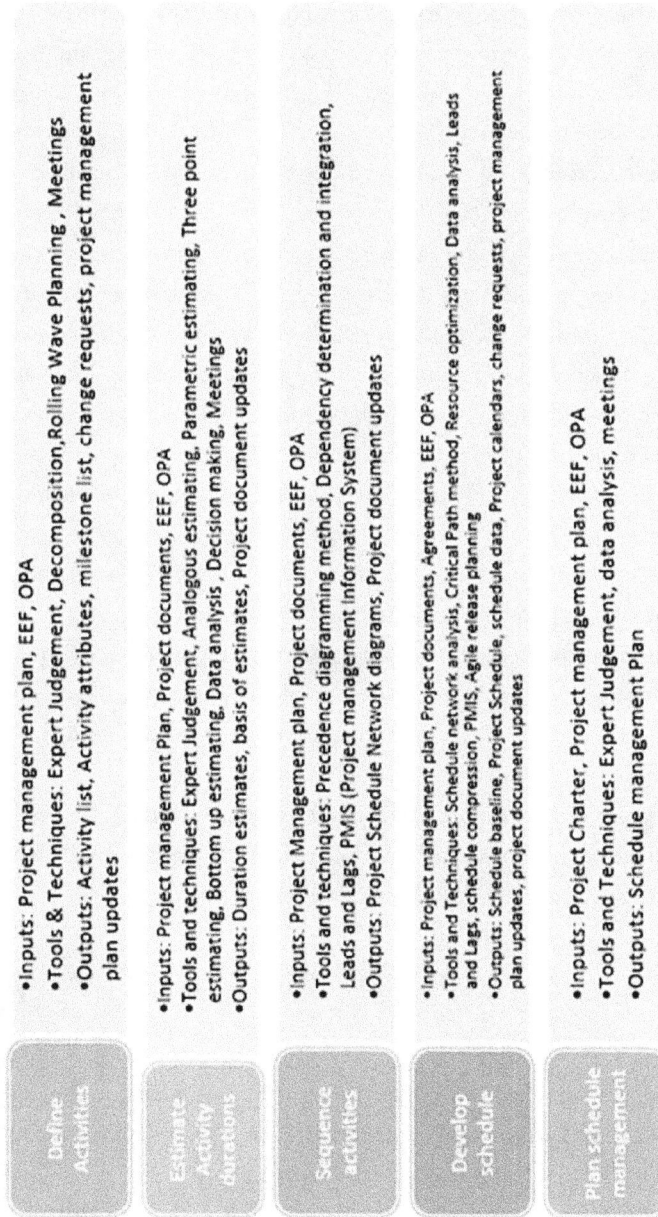

Figure 2.9 ITTO—Project lifecycle: Planning Schedule

2.2.3.1 Types of Estimates

The information provided in the Harvard Business Review article[11] suggests that managers in companies selling multiple products may be making decisions about multiple factors at once involving pricing, product mix, and process technology and so on. The situation may go out of control if it is based on distorted information. This situation highlights the importance of accurate estimation methods to support decision-making processes effectively.

There are different types of estimates which serve different needs and purposes. Analogous estimates are based on the ***same/similar activity***. {***Look out for the keyword highlighted***}. It is also known as ***Top-down estimating***, which uses historical data from ***previous*** projects. They are not as accurate as Bottom-up estimates. Bottom-up estimate is used when a high level of accuracy is needed in estimating cost or schedule. This is the most time-consuming estimate, so it should be ***avoided when time is a constraint***.

Bottom-up estimates would be using the lowest level of work package and summing up to get the aggregated cost/schedule.

Parametric estimates are based on parameters, **algorithms, or equations** between cost/schedule and some variable. For example, the cost of one equipment is 100K USD, and there are two equipment needed, so the total equipment cost would be 200K USD.

Three-point estimates, also known as **triangular estimates**, are based on the average of the costs/schedule. It is used when there is insufficient data from previous activity or less historical information.

$$\text{Three-point estimate} = \frac{\textit{optimistic duration} + \textit{Pessimistic duration} + \textit{Most likely duration}}{3}$$

where *Optimistic duration* is based on the best-case scenario, *pessimistic duration* is based on the worst-case scenario, and *Most likely duration* is the cost of activity based on realistic effort assessment.

Example: A team is working on a new project with a construction company, and there is no previous data available. SME suggests it can most likely take 15 days to complete, and another stakeholder group has mentioned it might take, in the worst case, 20 days and, in the best case,

10 days to complete the task. What is the estimated development duration based on the triangular estimate?

$$Answer: \frac{(15 + 20 + 10)}{3} = 15 \text{ days}$$

Fixed Formula Method: A technique for calculating earned value whereby a predetermined portion of the budget value allocated to a work package is attributed to the project's start milestone, with the remaining portion earmarked upon the completion of the work package.

Commonly used methods for estimating include **affinity groups/ Venn diagrams**, where we estimate things based on similar context, parameters, and measures.

Let's consider a Venn diagram representing three key quality metrics in a software development project: Functionality, Reliability, and Usability.

In this Venn diagram:

- *The circle labeled "Functionality" represents the features and capabilities of the software.*
- *The circle labeled "Reliability" represents the dependability and consistency of the software.*
- *The circle labeled "Usability" represents how user-friendly and easy the software is to use. The overlapping areas between circles represent the combined characteristics.*
- *The overlap between "Functionality" and "Reliability" represents features that are not only functional but also reliable.*
- *The overlap between "Reliability" and "Usability" represents features that are both reliable and user-friendly.*
- *The overlap between "Functionality" and "Usability" represents features that are functional and user-friendly.*

The center where all three circles overlap, labeled "Overall Quality," represents features that excel in terms of functionality, reliability, and usability, contributing to the highest quality. This Venn diagram visually illustrates how these quality metrics interrelate and contribute to the overall quality of the software product.

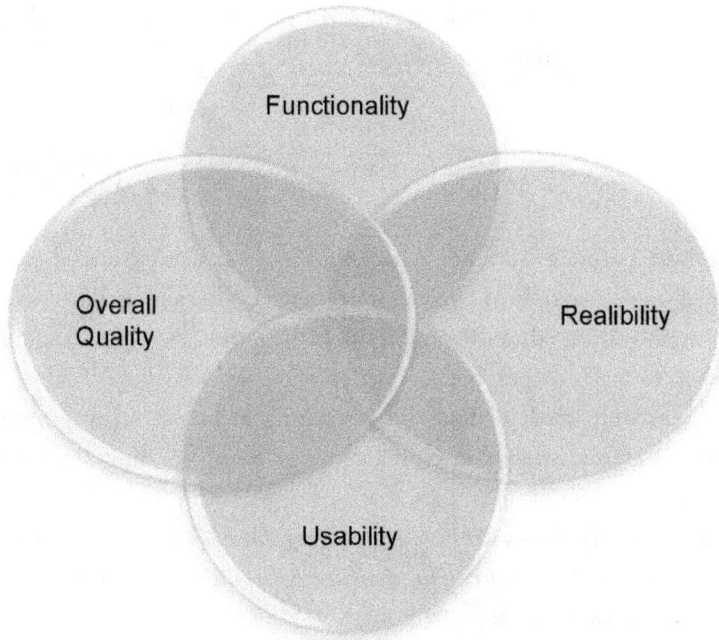

Figure 2.10 KPI—Key Quality Metrics

Single-point and multi-point estimating are two approaches used in project management to estimate project tasks or activities. Here are the key differences between them:

1. **Single-Point Estimating:**
   - **Definition:** Single-point estimating involves providing a single, specific estimate for a task or activity. It is essentially a "best guess" or most likely scenario.
   - **Nature:** It assumes that the most likely or average scenario will unfold and provides a single, fixed value as the estimate.
   - **Example:** Providing a project completion date based on the assumption that everything will proceed according to the plan without significant variations, Fibonacci.
2. **Multi-Point Estimating:**
   - **Definition:** Multi-point estimating involves considering a range of possible outcomes for a task or activity. It acknowledges uncertainty and variability.

- **Nature:** It provides a range of estimates, usually expressed as a minimum, maximum, and most likely value. This approach accounts for potential risks and uncertainties.
- **Example:** Estimating the duration of a task as a range (e.g., three to five days) to account for variations that may occur due to unforeseen circumstances.

Key Points

- Single-point estimating is simpler and quicker but may not account for uncertainties adequately.
- Multi-point estimating recognizes the inherent uncertainties in project work and provides a more comprehensive view of potential outcomes.
- Single-point estimates are often used when there's a high degree of confidence in the estimate.
- Multi-point estimates are beneficial when there's significant uncertainty and a range of possibilities needs to be considered.

PERT—Program Evaluation Review Technique, also known as **Beta estimate or weighted average**, is based on the Formula stated below. It is used when there is slight data from the previous activity, and we need a more accurate estimate, then it's best to go for the Beta technique.

$$PERT = \frac{\textit{optimistic duration} + \textit{Pessimistic duration} + \textit{Most likely duration} + (4 * \textit{Most likely duration})}{6}$$

2.2.3.2 Schedule Network Analysis

Network analysis would help in understanding what activity comes before/after which other activity. Let's say you are preparing pancakes, and then you can't eat the pancake before making the batter first. So, "eating" as an activity comes later and becomes the "successor," and "preparing the batter" becomes the "predecessor."

Critical Path Method analysis, also known as CPM, helps establish relationships between leading and lagging activities.

The critical path is the longest path in the Precedence Networking Diagram, where we can't afford to **slack.**

$$Float = 0 \ \{CRITICAL \ Path\}$$

Critical Path determines the shortest Possible Duration to complete the activity, and it's the most important path in any Project. **Bottlenecks** should be pre-analyzed to have zero slack on this path.

The Project Calendar identifies available working days and shifts for Scheduled Activities.

Figure 2.11 shows a **Work Breakdown Structure**. It can be defined as the procedure of breaking a work package into smaller work packages. It helps establish sequences of activities and Gantt chart.

$$\sum work \ packages \ or \ activities = Total \ Work$$

One such **important** activity in the sequence of activities would be defined as a milestone (the activities with a duration of zero).

- **Milestone:** It's a noteworthy point or event within a project, program, or portfolio.
- **Milestone Schedule:** This schedule highlights planned dates for significant milestones.
- **WBS Dictionary:** It's a document offering comprehensive information about each component in the work breakdown structure, including detailed deliverables, activities, and scheduling details. It serves as a detailed reference guide for project management.

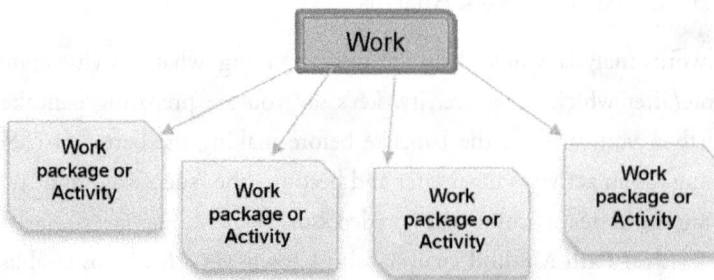

Figure 2.11 Work Breakdown Structure

Wideband Delphi is a consensus-based estimation technique used in project management. It is an enhancement of the traditional Delphi method, incorporating structured communication and group dynamics to achieve more accurate and reliable estimates.

Here's an overview of the Wideband Delphi process:

1. **Expert Input**
2. **Preparation for a Set of Estimation Items**
3. **Initial Individual Estimates**
4. **Collation of Estimates**
5. **Group Discussion**
6. **Revised Estimates**
7. **Consensus Building**
8. **Final Estimates**

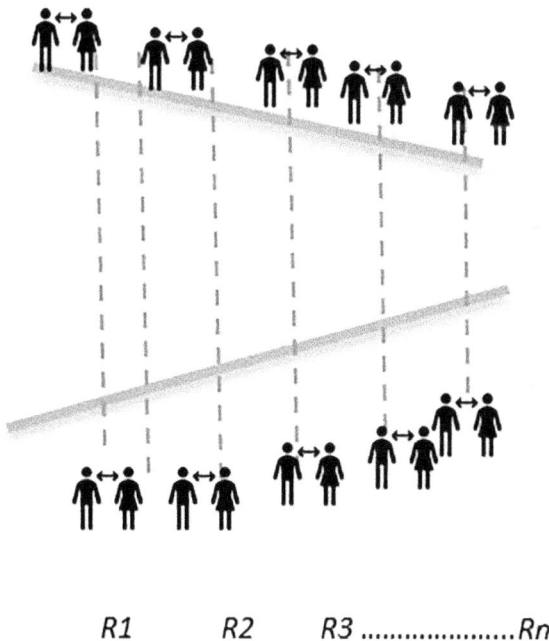

$$R1 \qquad R2 \qquad R3 \,.....................Rn$$

Figure 2.12 Multiple rounds (Round1 R1, R2, R3, ...Rn): Startbroad and then become more accurate

2.2.3.2.a Gantt Chart and Task Dependencies. It's a bar chart that can illustrate a Project Schedule [4]. Use it to draft the work packages individually, contributing to significant activity. Let's consider Figure 2.13, which shows how WBS can be broken to show relationships between Predecessor and Successor activities.

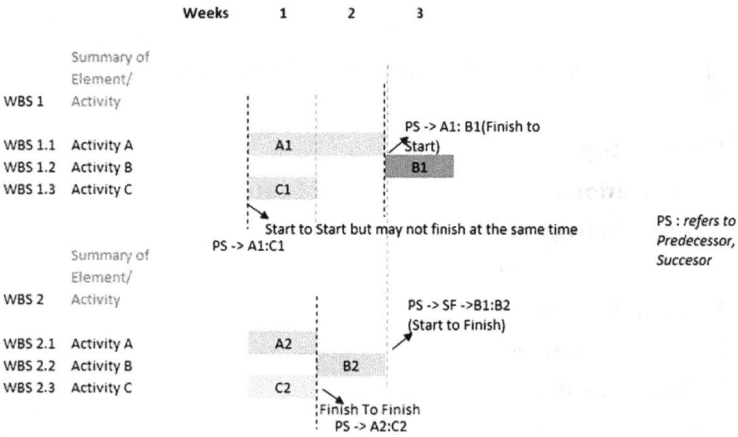

Figure 2.13 *Gantt chart and task dependencies*

Tip: Good way to learn and understand. PS refers to Predecessor (P) and Successor(S), which can be four combinations of S**F**/SS/F**F**/**F**S. Where S refers to Start, and **F** refers to Finish. P comes before S.

- **Finish to Start:** Successor activity cannot start until a Predecessor activity has finished. *Example*: Installing any equipment cannot start before all parts are ordered.
- **Start to Finish:** Successor activity cannot Finish if the Predecessor has not started yet. *Example*: Data migration to a new server must start before all old data can be deleted.
- **Finish to Finish:** Successor activity cannot finish until a Predecessor activity has finished. *Example*: Writing thesis can finish {can be called as completed} only after editing is finished {completed}.
- **Start to Start:** Successor activity can start only after the Predecessor activity has started. *Example*: E-mail draft can be started only when Outlook/Gmail is launched {started}.

2.2.3.2.b Resources Optimization.   When we are referring to resources generally, they include equipment, labor, materials, finances, expertise, time, and any other assets. For PMP scenario-based questions, the questions would mostly be around labor. There are certain instances that are not always under a Project Manager's control, such as new government regulations or laws or demand and supply chain disruptions that might affect deadlines on projects or any important milestones. In such situations, it's important to understand how one can optimize resources to get the best out of a painful situation.

Resources optimization can be Resource crashing, also known as schedule crashing. Other ways include Resource leveling, fast tracking, and resource smoothing. These are also known as options for accelerating project completion.

> **Resource crashing:** Can be done when you have some *reserves (contingency/management)* or any budget left or have the bandwidth to get the extra budget requirement approved from the sponsor. This is sometimes referred to as schedule crashing, where we can get new resources (temporary, permanent, or third party, depending upon the situation) to get work done. Usually, such situations may arise when there are not enough team members to complete the work in the given time or due to a lack of skills in the team, or extra work being offloaded due to some reason.
> *Note that hiring new team members from scratch can also take time, so this technique should be avoided when there is a time constraint or budget constraint. Look for subtle clues in the questions in the PMP exam, which might suggest a time/budget constraint.*
> **Resource Leveling:** As the term Leveling suggests, resources should be leveled amongst different activity groups that are performing a particular task. Sometimes, there are situations where more people are working on a task than needed or a situation where a particular resource is overloaded with multiple tasks unfairly. Then, there is a need to redistribute work.
> **Start and Finish dates can be adjusted** based on resources constraints with the goal of balancing resources and work. Thus, allowing tasks to be delayed, with the primary goal being fair work distribution. Usually, whatever float/slack is available can be used to level resources.

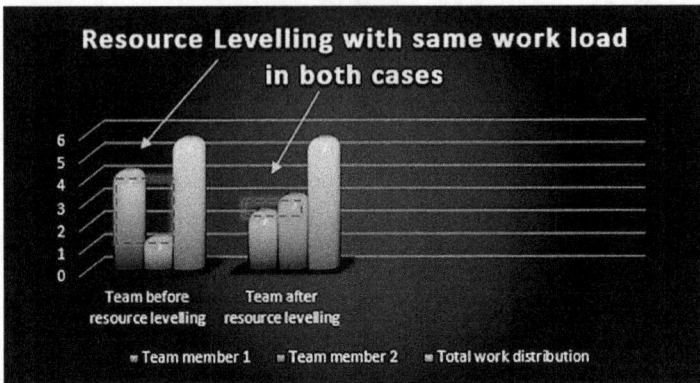

Figure 2.14 Resource leveling

In Figure 2.13, the workload was quite uneven between two team members. After resource leveling, it's almost ~equal between team members 1 and 2.

Resource Smoothing: This is also used whenever there is an uneven allocation of resources. It can be used after resource-leveling is completed, but **this optimization technique can't change the project end date**. Extra float can be used, and activities may be delayed within their free and total float.
Note that Critical Path doesn't change in any condition, and resource requirements don't have to exceed the pre-defined limits.
Fast Tracking: This process involves doing activities in parallel. Not all activities can be done in parallel unless there is a dependency such that one can start only after the predecessor has finished. However, if they are not interdependent, doing activities in parallel can help accelerate project completion.

2.2.3.2.c Critical Path Method and Precedence Network Diagram/Precedence Diagram Method (PDM)/Activity on Node (AON)

Early start	Duration	Early Finish
	Activity Name	
Late Start	Total Float	Late Finish

Figure 2.15 Representation of an Activity Node in PDM

$$Float = LS - ES$$

$$Float = LF - EF$$

Consider a construction project with the following activities:

Table 2.2 Task activity representation with dependencies

Activity	Duration (weeks)	Dependencies
Task 1	X1	None
Task 2	X2	Task 1
Task 3	X3	Task 1
Task 4	X4	Task 2, Task 3
Task 5	X5	Task 4
Task 6	X6	Task 3
Task 7	X7	Task 4, Task 6

Using the provided data, create a network diagram and determine the Critical Path[5] for the project.

Solution: To begin, let's represent each activity as a node in the network diagram, connected by arrows to show their dependencies. Afterward, we'll calculate the Critical Path.[2]

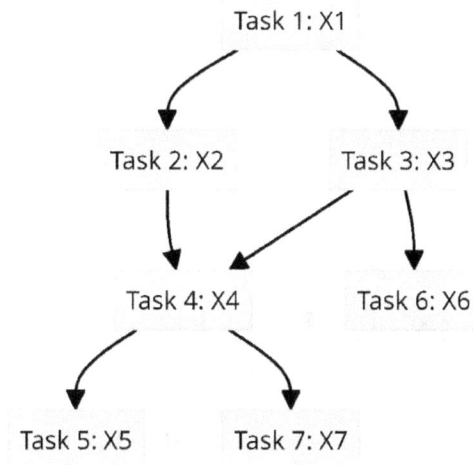

Figure 2.16 Representation of path diagram

Next, we'll calculate the earliest start (ES), earliest finish (EF), latest start (LS), latest finish (LF), and float for each activity.

Table 2.3 ES, EF, LS, LF float calculations

Task	Early Start (ES)	Early Finish (EF)	Late Start (LS)	Late Finish (LF)	Float
X1	0	X1	0	X1	0
X2	X1	X1 + X2	X1	X1 + X2	X2
X3	0	X3	0	X3	0
X4	X1 + X2	X1 + X2 + X3 + X4	X1 + X2	X1 + X2 + X3 + X4	X4 – X2
X5	X1 + X2 + X3 + X4	X1 + X2 + X3 + X4 + X5	X1 + X2 + X3 + X4	X1 + X2 + X3 + X4 + X5	X5
X6	0	X3 + X6	0	X3 + X6	X3 + X6
X7	X1 + X2 + X3 + X4	X1 + X2 + X3 + X4 + X7	X1 + X2 + X3 + X4	X1 + X2 + X3 + X4 + X7	X7

Finally, we identify the critical path, which consists of activities with zero float, indicating they must be completed on time to avoid delaying the project. The critical path for this project is Task 1—Task 2—Task 4—Task 5.

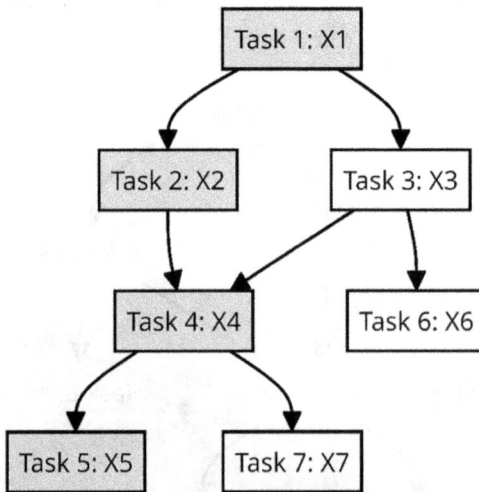

Figure 2.17 Representation of critical path in task diagram

Some other important keywords for the exam are as follows:

Logical Relationship can be defined as a connection or sequential link between two tasks or between a task and a significant milestone.

Proximate to Critical Activity, also referred to as Near-Critical Activity, can be identified as having minimal margin for delay, typically determined through expert evaluation.

Near-Critical Path is a series of tasks with limited flexibility, which, if further constrained, would become a critical path section for the project.[2]

Network Logic can be referred to as the entirety of task interdependencies depicted in a project schedule diagram, whereas a **Network Trail/Path** denotes a sequence of tasks interconnected by logical relationships in the diagram, with a **Node** marking the juncture.

Flexible Margins/Free Float: the period within which an activity can be postponed without impacting subsequent tasks' early start or violating any schedule constraints.

Lag: the duration by which a subsequent task is delayed in relation to a preceding one.

Late Finish Date: the latest feasible moment for completing an incomplete task, considering the project's logic, endpoint, and constraints.

Late Start Date: the latest feasible moment for commencing an incomplete task, considering the project's logic, endpoint, and constraints.

Lead: the period by which a subsequent task can be expedited in relation to a preceding one.

Backward Pass, also referred to as Retroactive Tracing: a method within critical path analysis for deducing late start and late finish dates by working backward from the project's endpoint.

Forward Pass/Progressive Tracing: a technique within critical path analysis for determining early start and early finish dates by moving forward from the project's initiation date or a specified juncture.

Early Finish Date: the earliest feasible time for concluding an incomplete task, considering the project's logic, reference date, and constraints.

Early Start Date: the earliest feasible time for commencing an incomplete task, considering the project's logic, reference date, and constraints.

Duration: the overall time necessary for completing a task or component of the work breakdown structure, measured in hours, days, or weeks.

2.2.4 Plan Cost

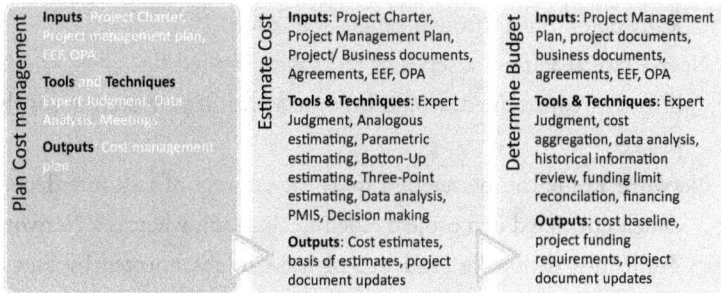

Plan Cost management	Estimate Cost	Determine Budget
Inputs: Project Charter, Project management plan, EEF, OPA **Tools** and **Techniques** Expert Judgment, Data Analysis, Meetings **Outputs** Cost management plan	**Inputs**: Project Charter, Project Management Plan, Project/ Business documents, Agreements, EEF, OPA **Tools & Techniques**: Expert Judgment, Analogous estimating, Parametric estimating, Botton-Up estimating, Three-Point estimating, Data analysis, PMIS, Decision making **Outputs**: Cost estimates, basis of estimates, project document updates	**Inputs**: Project Management Plan, project documents, business documents, agreements, EEF, OPA **Tools & Techniques**: Expert Judgment, cost aggregation, data analysis, historical information review, funding limit reconcilation, financing **Outputs**: cost baseline, project funding requirements, project document updates

Figure 2.18 ITTO—Project lifecycle: Planning cost[9]

The types of estimates being used as tools are similar to those we studied in section 2.2.3.

A crucial aspect worth noting for exam preparation includes understanding Earned Value Management, establishing cost baselines, conducting S curve analysis, exploring various estimation techniques, and considering project selection criteria like NPV and ROI. Rest assured, we'll delve into each of these topics sequentially, making it quick and easy for you to grasp.

2.2.4.1 Types of Cost

Various expenses[6] contribute to establishing a project's cost baseline and total budget. The cost baseline approximates the overall project expenditure, encompassing all allocated funds for project execution. Typically represented by an S curve, depicting cumulative project costs over time, the cost baseline incorporates contingency reserves but does not account for management reserves. It is also known as control account cost.[9]

In summary,

1. Project Budget = Estimated Project Costs + Additional Reserves for Management Purposes[1]
2. Estimated[6] Project Costs = Sum of Estimated Costs for Individual Work Packages + Additional Reserves for Unforeseen Expenses[1]

3. Estimated Costs for Individual Work Packages = Estimated Costs for Specific Project Activities + Additional Reserves for Unexpected Costs[1]

Contingency Reserves: Allotted time or funds within the schedule or cost baseline to address identified risks with proactive response plans.[2]

Management Reserves: Additional time or funds set aside by management beyond the schedule or cost baseline to address unforeseen tasks within the project's scope.[2]

Cost Baseline[3]: The approved version of work package cost estimates and contingency reserves, subject to formal change control procedures, serving as the benchmark for comparing actual results.

Cost Management Plan: A segment of the project or program management plan, outlining strategies for planning, organizing, and overseeing costs.[3]

Control Account: A pivotal management checkpoint where project scope, budget, actual expenses, and schedule are fused and assessed against earned value for performance evaluation.[3]

Contingency Plan: A comprehensive document outlining actions to be taken by the project team in response to predefined trigger events.[4]

Configuration Management System: A set of protocols utilized to monitor project artifacts and regulate modifications to these artifacts.[4]

Code of Accounts: A numbering scheme employed to uniquely identify each element of the work breakdown structure.[4]

2.2.4.2 Project Selection Methods/Project Management Formulas

Project selection is a critical phase in project management, determining which initiatives to undertake based on various criteria and methodologies. Understanding and applying appropriate project selection methods ensure that resources are allocated efficiently, leading to successful project outcomes. Below are some commonly used project selection methods:

Net Present Value[6] **(NPV)** assesses the present value of all future cash flows[8] over the lifespan of an investment, discounted to its current value. It is calculated as the difference between the sum of present values of all future cash inflows and the initial cash outflow. Projects with a positive NPV are deemed financially viable and are typically accepted.[5]

Example: Consider two projects with the following NPV values:

- Project A: NPV = $50,000
- Project B: NPV = $30,000

In this case, Project A would be preferred due to its higher NPV.

Internal Rate of Return (IRR) is the discount rate at which the NPV of a project equals zero. It represents the project's expected rate of return and helps evaluate an investment's attractiveness. Projects with an IRR greater than the predetermined threshold are usually accepted.

Example: Project X has an IRR of 15 percent, while Project Y has an IRR of 10 percent. Since both IRR values exceed the company's required rate of return of 12 percent, both projects are acceptable.[6]

Benefit Cost Ratio (BCR)/Cost Benefit Analysis (CBA) compares the sum of present values of all cash inflows to the project's cash outflow. A ratio greater than one indicates that the benefits outweigh the costs, making the project favorable for implementation.[7]

Example: Project P has a BCR of 1.5, meaning that for every $1 invested, $1.50 worth of benefits is expected. Thus, Project P is considered economically viable.

Return on Investment (ROI) measures the profitability of a project by comparing the average income generated to the average investment made. Projects with an ROI exceeding a predefined threshold are considered financially viable.[8]

Example: Project Q generates an average income of $100,000 per year with an initial investment of $500,000. Therefore, its ROI is ($100,000/$500,000) * 100% = 20%. Since this exceeds the company's minimum ROI requirement of 15 percent, Project Q is acceptable.

Payback Period represents the time taken for the initial investment to be recouped through the project's generated cash inflows. Projects with a payback period shorter than the predetermined threshold are typically accepted.[7]

Example: Project R requires an initial investment of $200,000 and generates an annual cash inflow of $50,000. Its payback period is four years ($200,000/$50,000). If the company's payback period threshold is 3 years, Project R would not be accepted.

Table 2.4 Project selection methods

Method	Criteria	Decision
Present Value	Positive value	Select
	Negative value	Reject
Internal Rate of Return	Exceeds threshold	Select
	Below threshold	Reject
Benefit Cost Ratio	BCR > 1	Select
	BCR < 1	Reject
Return on Investment	ROI > Threshold	Select
Payback Period	Below threshold	Select
	Above threshold	Reject

2.2.4.3 Earned Value Management

An integrated project management approach utilizing the earned value concept employs a time-phased budget baseline to analyze actual versus planned schedules and costs, known as **Earned Value Management (EVM)**.[3] In essence, EVM assesses the percentage of project completion concerning time and cost management, facilitating comparisons with the **cost and schedule baselines**.

Tip: This topic is anticipated to feature at least one, if not multiple, question in examinations.

Apportioned Effort[20] refers to an activity that allocates effort proportionally across specific discrete tasks rather than being divisible into distinct efforts. It's worth noting that Apportioned Effort is one of three types of activities within Earned Value Management[9] (EVM) used for measuring work performance. Additionally, we will delve into discrete effort and the level of effort during our discussion.

Note that when we talk about effort, we mean labor units. With reference to labor, we mean resources. So,

Effort α (*Directly proportional*) labor units $\frac{1}{\alpha}$ (*Inversely Proportional*) Duration

If we have more people working on an activity, then the duration to complete that activity would be less as effort increases with labor units.

Earned Value (EV) represents the proportion of work completed multiplied by its original budget. It signifies the percentage of the initial budget earned through actual work accomplished. Previously known as **BCWP** (budgeted cost of the work performed).

Planned Value (PV), also referred to as the time-phased baseline, denotes the projected value of scheduled work. It constitutes an approved cost estimate of scheduled resources in a cumulative time-phased baseline (BCWS—budgeted cost of the work scheduled).

Actual Cost (AC) reflects the incurred cost for work completed during a specified timeframe (**ACWP**—actual cost of the work performed).

Budget at Completion (BAC) sums up all budgets allocated for planned work.

Cost Performance Index (CPI) gauges the cost efficiency of budgeted resources by comparing the earned value to the actual cost.

Cost Variance (CV) indicates the budget deficit or surplus at a given point, derived from the difference between earned value and actual cost.

Schedule Performance Index (SPI) assesses schedule efficiency by comparing earned value to planned value.

Schedule Variance (SV) measures schedule performance as the difference between earned and planned value.

Variance Analysis is a method for identifying the cause and extent of deviations between baseline and actual performance.

Variance at Completion (VAC) forecasts the budget surplus or deficit, expressed as the variance between the budget at completion and the estimated completion cost.

To-Complete Performance Index (TCPI) indicates the cost performance required to meet a specified management goal, calculated as the ratio of the cost to finish outstanding work to the remaining budget.

Estimate at Complete (EAC) estimates total costs at project completion, encompassing costs incurred to date plus revised estimates for pending work.

ETC (Estimated Time to Complete) signifies the projected duration needed to finish pending work.

Cost of Change refers to the increased expense associated with identifying defects later in the project, emphasizing the importance of early detection in cost management.

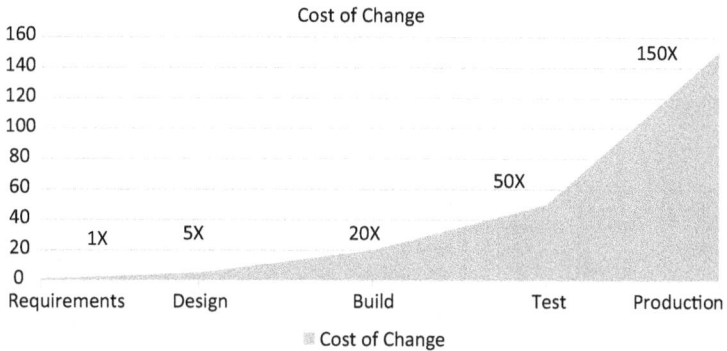

Figure 2.19 *Graphical representation of variances of cost and also referred to as the cost of change curve*

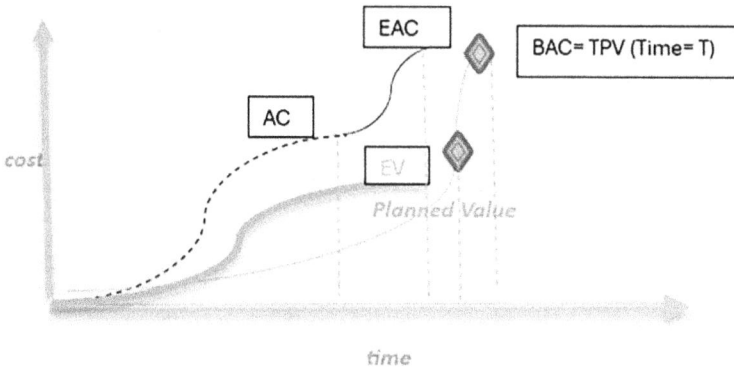

Figure 2.20 *Earned value analysis*

Here are some tricks and formulas on which you can expect basic numerical in examination.

Table 2.5 *EVM terms*

Term	Definition
PV	Estimated schedule at time "t" when total time is "T" and schedule at "T" is BAC
CPI	Cost Performance Index = EV/AC
SPI	Schedule Performance Index = EV/PV
CV	Cost Variance = EV – AC
SV	Schedule Variance = EV – PV
TCPI	To-Complete Performance Index
CPI, CV, SPI, SV < 1	Indicates over budget and behind schedule

(*Continued*)

Table 2.5 (Continued)

Term	Definition
CPI, SPI > 1	Indicates under budget and ahead of schedule
TCPI < 1	Indicates good progress, TCPI > 1 indicates bad progress
CPI = 1, SPI = 1	Most ideal case
Notes	Positive CV indicates project is under budget, positive SV indicates project is ahead of schedule
PV	Planned Value (BCWS = Budgeted Cost of Work Scheduled)
AC	Actual Cost (ACWP = Actual Cost of Work Performed)
EV	Earned Value (BCWP = Budgeted Cost of Work Performed)

Easy tip to learn this formula.

- *The formula starts with EV.*
- *If a formula is related to variance {which means difference} CV, SV, then the next symbol would be a minus sign.*
- *When dealing with performance metrics such as CPI and SPI, if the formula involves division, the subsequent symbol is the division sign. In the formulas for CV and CPI, AC is included, whereas in the formulas for SV and SPI, PV is incorporated.*
- *In the exam, you will often be presented with a scenario that requires you to work out one set of figures before working out a final set of calculations. For example, you may be asked to work out EAC using CPI Or SPI, whatever is given, and then use that to calculate and so on.*
- *Writing down all the formulas you know and then checking what fits best to the "given and asked" in question is the best way to solve a numerical problem.*

Predictive analysis, also referred to as **Forecasting,** involves leveraging past time and cost performance data to anticipate future project outcomes. Utilizing metrics like CV, SV, CPI, and SPI enables project managers to estimate the anticipated project cost at completion, providing insight into the financial resources needed to finalize the project.

Table 2.6 Formulas

Formula	Description
EAC = BAC/CPI	Estimate at Completion based on Cost Performance Index (CPI)
EAC = AC + ETC	Estimate at Completion based on Actual Cost (AC) and Estimated to Complete (ETC)
EAC = AC + (BAC – EV)	Estimate at Completion based on Actual Cost (AC), Budget at Completion (BAC), and Earned Value (EV)
$EAC = AC + (\dfrac{BAC - EV}{CPI \times SPI})$	Estimate at Completion based on Actual Cost (AC), Budget at Completion (BAC), Earned Value (EV), Cost Performance Index (CPI), and Schedule Performance Index (SPI)
ETC = EAC – AC	Estimated to Complete based on Estimate at Completion (EAC) and Actual Cost (AC)
VAC = BAC – EAC	Variance at Completion based on Budget at Completion (BAC) and Estimate at Completion (EAC)
$TCPI = \dfrac{BAC - EV}{BAC - AC}$	To-Complete Performance Index based on Budget at Completion (BAC), Earned Value (EV), and Actual Cost (AC)
PV = % completed (planned) × task budget	Planned Value based on percentage completed and task budget
EV = % Completed × task budget	Earned Value based on percentage completed and task budget
CPI = EV/AC	Cost Performance Index based on Earned Value (EV) and Actual Cost (AC)
SPI = EV/PV	Schedule Performance Index based on Earned Value (EV) and Planned Value (PV)

Here's an additional example included in the table:

Example	Calculation
PV = 20% x $10000	Planned Value (PV) = 20% x $10000 = $2000
CPI and SPI	Given: EV = 65% x $10K, AC = $10K
	CPI = EV/AC = (0.65 x $10K)/$10K = 0.65
	SPI = EV/PV = (0.65 x $10K)/(0.80 x $10K) = 0.8125

Example: You are the PM on a construction project with 10 identical offices. You expect to spend $50K per office to complete the work and take 20 months to finish. You are 12 months into the work and have completed five offices and spent $310K in total. Use this information to calculate the following?

Budget at Complete

We know the individual cost, so BAC should be just linear multiplication BAC = 10 offices × $50K each =$500K.

Actual Cost

You have spent $310K in total, so the actual cost is known to you.

Planned Value

You are 12 months into a 20-month work program, so you have planned to have created value equal to 12/20 or 60 percent of TPV or BAC. Hence PV = 60% × 500K = $300K.

Earned Value

You have built five offices, and the value of each is $50K, so earned value is 5 × $50K = $250K.

Cost Variance

This should be simple as now we know EV and AC, and the difference is –$60k.

CPI

EV/AC = 0.81. Now, when CPI is less than 1, which indicates an unfavorable condition, it suggests that the project is going over budget and, in this case, you might not be able to use methods like resource/schedule crashing as we are already over budget unless approved otherwise when asked from sponsor. Also note that going to sponsors or executives for budget increases is usually the last resort (any escalation is usually the last resort to higher management, sponsor, or PMO unless no options are left otherwise). PMs should be good at understanding such cases on their own and solving them using their leadership and management skills. Fast tracking (doing things in parallel or resource optimization) can be helpful.

2.2.5 Plan Quality

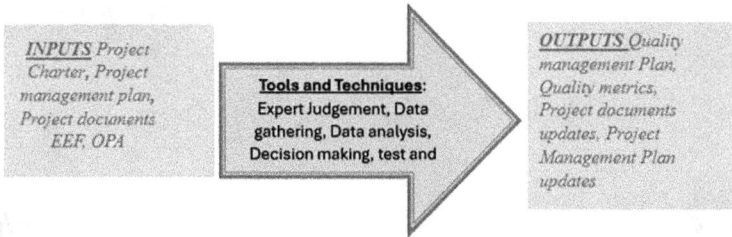

Figure 2.21 ITTO—Project lifecycle: planning quality[9]

2.2.5.1 Quality Terminologies

Quality metrics[15] are measures or KPIs (Key Performance Indicators) used to assess the quality of a product, process, or project. These metrics are essential in various industries to ensure that the final output meets the desired standards and specifications. Quality metrics are often employed in fields such as manufacturing, software development, project management, healthcare, and more. Here are some common types of quality metrics.[15]

1. **Defect Density:** This metric calculates the number of defects or errors identified per unit of measurement, such as lines of code, components, or features. It helps evaluate the overall product quality.
2. **Customer Satisfaction:** This metric gauges the level of satisfaction among end-users or customers. It may involve surveys, feedback forms, or other methods to collect customer opinions and experiences.
3. **Failure Rate:** This metric assesses the frequency at which a product, system, or component fails over a given period. It is commonly used in reliability and maintenance assessments.
4. **Test Coverage:** In software development, test coverage measures the extent to which the code has been tested. It helps identify areas that need additional testing to ensure comprehensive coverage.
5. **Lead Time:** This metric measures the time it takes to complete a process or deliver a product. It is crucial for evaluating efficiency and timeliness in project management and manufacturing.

6. **Cost of Quality (CoQ):** CoQ[15] assesses the total cost incurred by an organization to ensure product quality. It includes prevention costs, appraisal costs, internal failure costs, and external failure costs.

$$CoQ = COPE \ (Cost \ of \ Poor \ Execution) + CONC \ (Cost \ of$$
$$Non\text{-}Conformance)$$

CONC includes defectivity, costs internal to the organization. Reworks can help here. COPE: includes corrective/preventive action, appraisal costs, and the costs that come from customer returns/repairs.

It's always recommended to incorporate quality from the beginning as the cost to quality increases as much as it's near to the end product. Create a culture amongst team members in the company to instill the commitment to quality in processes as well as products. "Quality" is "every team member's responsibility."

Managing quality is also referred to as quality assurance.

7. **Compliance Rate:** This metric evaluates the extent to which a product or process complies with industry standards, regulations, or internal guidelines.

8. **Rework Rate:** Rework rate measures the percentage of work that needs to be redone or corrected. A high rework rate indicates potential issues in the development or manufacturing process.[15]

9. **Cycle Time:** This metric tracks the time it takes to complete a specific task or process, from initiation to completion. It is valuable for identifying bottlenecks and improving overall efficiency.

10. **First-Pass Yield (FPY):** FPY measures the percentage of products or services that meet quality standards without the need for rework or additional processing.

These metrics help organizations monitor, control, and improve the quality of their products and processes, ultimately contributing to customer satisfaction and business success. The specific metrics chosen may vary depending on the industry, project, or organizational goals.

2.2.5.2 Data Representation Techniques Using Quality Control

In quality control,[16] effective data representation techniques are crucial for analyzing and interpreting information related to the quality of products or processes. Various techniques are employed to visually represent data, making it easier for stakeholders to understand patterns, trends, and anomalies. Here are some common data representation techniques [17] used in quality control:

1. **Control Charts:** Control charts, also known as Shewhart charts or process-behavior charts, display how a process variable changes over time. They have a central line representing the mean and upper and lower control limits to identify variations outside the acceptable range.
2. **Histograms:** Histograms are graphical representations of the distribution of a set of data. They provide a visual summary of the data's central tendency, spread, and shape, helping to identify patterns and abnormalities.
3. **Scatter Plots:** Scatter plots show the relationship between two variables. In quality control, they are often used to identify correlations between process variables and detect any potential cause-and-effect relationships.
4. **Box-and-Whisker Plots (Boxplots):** Boxplots display the distribution of a dataset and highlight the central tendency and spread of the data. They are useful for comparing multiple sets of data and identifying outliers.
5. **Pareto Charts:** Pareto charts are bar charts that display the frequency of problems or defects in descending order. They help identify the most significant issues, allowing organizations to prioritize improvement efforts.
6. **Fishbone Diagrams (Ishikawa or Cause-and-Effect Diagrams):** Fishbone diagrams visually represent potential causes of a problem. They help quality control teams identify root causes by categorizing factors contributing to defects or issues.
7. **Run Charts:** Run charts display data points over time and help identify trends, patterns, or shifts in a process. They are useful for tracking changes and assessing the effectiveness of process improvements.
8. **Scatter Matrix:** A scatter matrix, or scatterplot matrix, is a grid of scatter plots that allows for simultaneously visualizing relationships between multiple variables. It is beneficial when examining multivariate data.

9. **Heat Maps:** Heat maps use colors to represent the magnitude of values in a matrix. In quality control, they can be used to identify areas of a process that require attention based on the intensity of certain characteristics.

10. **Capability Indices (e.g., Cp, Cpk):** Capability indices quantify the ability of a process to produce output within specified limits. These indices are often represented numerically but can be visually displayed for easier interpretation.

The choice of data representation technique depends on the nature of the data and the specific objectives of the quality control analysis. Utilizing a combination of these techniques provides a comprehensive view of the quality-related information and facilitates informed decision making.

2.2.5.3 Methods to Improve Quality

Improving quality is a continuous process that involves identifying and implementing measures to enhance products, services, and processes. Here are several methods and strategies commonly employed to improve quality:[17]

1. **Define Clear Quality Standards**
   - Establish clear and measurable quality standards for products, services, and processes.
   - Clearly communicate these standards to all stakeholders involved in the production or delivery process.

2. **Employee Training and Development**
   - Provide training programs to enhance the skills and knowledge of employees.
   - Ensure that employees understand the importance of quality and are equipped to meet established standards.

3. **Continuous Improvement (Kaizen)**
   - Adopt a culture of continuous improvement where employees are encouraged to identify and implement small, incremental improvements regularly.

- Foster a mindset that seeks efficiency gains and quality enhancements in all aspects of the organization.

4. **Quality Control Tools and Techniques**
   - Implement statistical process control (SPC) and other quality control tools to monitor and control variations in processes.
   - Use tools such as control charts, Pareto analysis, and Ishikawa diagrams to identify and address quality issues.

5. **Customer Feedback and Engagement**
   - Gather feedback from customers to understand their expectations and perceptions of quality.
   - Engage with customers to identify areas for improvement and prioritize initiatives based on customer needs.

6. **Supplier Quality Management**
   - Collaborate closely with suppliers to ensure the quality of incoming materials and components.
   - Implement supplier performance metrics and conduct regular assessments to monitor and improve supplier quality.

7. **Process Standardization**
   - Standardize processes to reduce variations and errors.
   - Develop and document standard operating procedures (SOPs) to ensure consistency in operations.

8. **Technology Integration**
   - Implement advanced technologies such as automation, artificial intelligence, and data analytics to enhance the precision and efficiency of processes.
   - Utilize technology for real-time monitoring and early detection of quality issues.

9. **Cross-functional Collaboration**
   - Encourage collaboration between different departments or teams within the organization.
   - Foster communication and teamwork to address quality challenges collectively.

10. **Root Cause Analysis**
    - Conduct thorough root cause analysis to identify the underlying reasons for quality issues.

- Address the root causes to prevent the recurrence of similar problems in the future.

11. **Benchmarking**
    - Benchmark against industry leaders and best practices to identify areas where improvements can be made.
    - Learn from successful organizations and adapt their best practices to enhance your own processes.

12. **Invest in Quality Management Systems (QMS)**
    - Implement QMS frameworks such as ISO 9001[16] to establish a systematic approach to quality management.
    - Regularly audit and review QMS processes to ensure compliance and effectiveness.

13. **Incentive Programs**
    - Introduce incentive programs to reward employees for achieving and maintaining high-quality standards.
    - Recognize and celebrate quality achievements to motivate continuous improvement efforts.

By combining these methods and customizing them to fit an organization's specific needs, businesses can build a robust quality improvement strategy that contributes to long-term success.

2.2.5.4 Quality Management Tools

RCA (Root Cause Analysis), 5 Whys, Ishikawa (Fishbone) Diagram, and Lean[17] Six Sigma are all methodologies[17] and tools used in quality management and process improvement.[18] They are interconnected in their approach to identifying, analyzing, and resolving organizational issues.

2.2.5.5 Differences Between Verification and Validation

In project management, particularly within the context of the Project Management Institute's (PMI)[19] processes, the terms "verified deliverables," "verification," and "validation" are used to describe different stages of ensuring project success and meeting requirements.

2.2.6 Plan Resources

Resources can be human, labor, equipment, and materials. The management plan for resources guides on how project resources should be categorized, allocated, managed, and released.

Table 2.7 ITTO—Project lifecycle: Planning resources[9]

Plan Resource Management	Estimate Activity Resources
Inputs: Project Charter, Project management Plan, Project documents, EEF, OPA	Inputs: Project management plan, project documents, EEF, OPA
Tools and techniques: Expert Judgment, Data representation, organizational theory, meetings	Tools and techniques: Expert judgment, bottom-up estimating, analogous estimating, parametric estimating, data analysis, PMIS-Project management Information System, meetings
Outputs: Resource management plan, team charter, project document updates	Outputs: Resource requirements, Basis of estimates, Resource breakdown structure, project document updates

Let's try to understand the resource breakdown structure, but before that, let's briefly recap the **Organizational Breakdown Structure** is a hierarchical representation of the project organization, which illustrates the relationship between project activities and the organizational units that will perform those activities[9] whereas **Organizational Enabler is a kind of** structural, cultural, technological, or human-resource practice that the performing organization can use to achieve strategic objectives.[9] Similar to a work breakdown structure we have **Resource Breakdown Structure**. It is a hierarchical representation of resources by category and type.[21]

Some of the other terms that you might hear often in the examination question types are:

Resource Calendar—is a calendar that identifies the working days and shifts upon which each specific resource is available.[21] **Resource Management Plan**: A component of the project management plan that describes how project resources are acquired, allocated, monitored, and controlled.[9]

Team Charter is a kind of **social contract/social agreement** for the team, by the team. It establishes a team's values, agreements, and operating guidelines and lays out the expectations and behaviors.[9]

Project managers should always create an environment that facilitates teamwork and continuously motivates the team by providing challenging opportunities. A project manager **should never challenge** the team to do things; instead, **stand up** for the team's views.[20]

2.2.6.1 Five Stages of Team Development

We will discuss models and artifacts in different sections at a later stage in detail. For now, one important model **is the Tuckman Ladder[22] Model** (Figure 2.19), which helps with stages of team development. According to this, there are **five stages** of team development known as **Forming > Storming > Norming > Performing > Adjourning.**

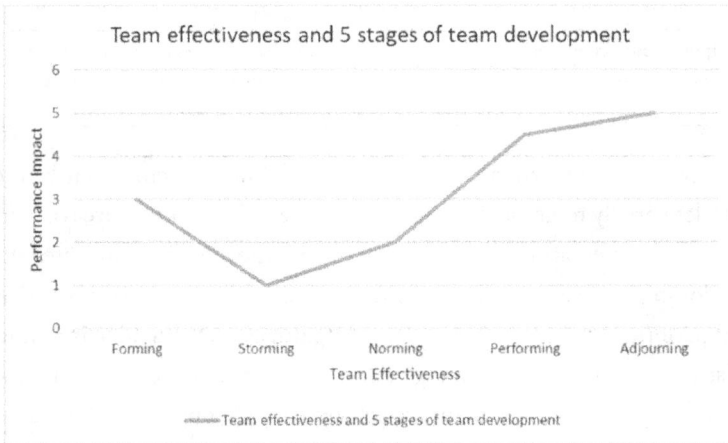

Figure 2.22 Tuckman ladder[22] model

1. **Forming**
   - In this initial stage, team members are polite and get acquainted. They often seek guidance and direction from a leader and tend to avoid conflict.
2. **Storming**
   - During the storming stage, team members may start to express their individual opinions and challenge the team's goals and objectives. Conflict and tension can arise as individuals with different working styles or perspectives clash.

3. Norming

- In the norming stage, the team begins to resolve its conflicts, establish common goals, and develop norms or guidelines for behavior. Team members start to appreciate each other's strengths and work more cohesively.

4. Performing

- The performing stage is characterized by high levels of cooperation, collaboration, and productivity. The team has established effective processes, and members work together toward achieving the team's goals. There is a sense of unity and shared vision.

  Additionally, in the 1970s, Tuckman added a fifth stage:

5. Adjourning (or Mourning)

- In this stage, the team is completing its tasks, and there is a sense of closure. Team members reflect on accomplishments and experiences. This stage is particularly relevant for temporary project teams that disband after completing their work.

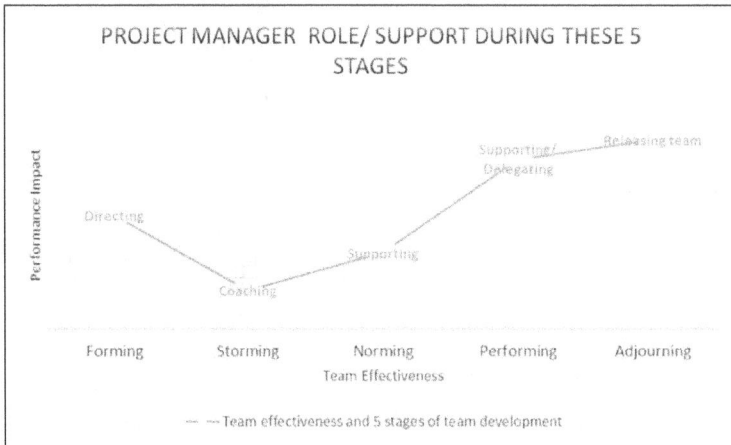

Figure 2.23 Project manager's role during five stages

2.2.6.2 RACI

RACI[23] Chart/RACI assignment matrix is one of the tools widely used for resource/stakeholder management.

A RACI matrix, also known as a Responsibility Assignment Matrix, is a project management tool used to define and communicate the roles and responsibilities for tasks and deliverables in a project or business process. RACI stands for Responsible, Accountable, Consulted, and Informed, which represent the four key roles associated with each task.

Here is what each role in the RACI matrix represents:

- **Responsible (R):** The person or people responsible for performing the task or activity. They are the "doers."
- **Accountable (A):** The person who is ultimately answerable for the task's completion or the decision-making process. This person is often the one held accountable if something goes wrong. There should be only one "A" for each task.
- **Consulted (C):** Individuals or groups who need to provide input or expertise before the task can be completed. These are the subject matter experts or stakeholders who are consulted for their insights.
- **Informed (I):** Individuals or groups who need to be kept in the loop about the task's progress but don't need to be directly involved in its completion.

Here's a simple example of a RACI matrix for a project task:

Table 2.8 RACI matrix

Task	Project Manager	Team Leader	Subject Expert	Team Member 1	Team Member 2
Task A	A	R	C	I	I
Task B	R	A	C	I	I
Task C	C	A	R	I	I
Task D	I	I	C	R	A

In this example:

- **Task A:** The Project Manager is ultimately accountable (A) for the task's completion. The Team Leader is responsible (R) for performing the task, and both the Subject Expert and Team Members 1 and 2 are consulted (C).

- **Task B:** The Team Leader is responsible (R), and the Project Manager is accountable (A). The Subject Expert is consulted (C).
- **Task C:** The Subject Expert is responsible (R), and the Project Manager is accountable (A). Team Members 1 and 2 are consulted (C).
- **Task D:** Team Member 1 is responsible (R), and the Team Leader is accountable (A). The Subject Expert is consulted (C).

This matrix helps clarify roles and responsibilities, reducing confusion and ensuring everyone knows their part in the project or process.

Stakeholder analysis can also be understood by using the Power versus Interest matrix. If a stakeholder has High interest, they must be managed closely and kept informed. *Say you have team members A, B, C, and D, and based on their power and interest, you can score as follows and decide who needs to be managed closely and paid the maximum attention.*

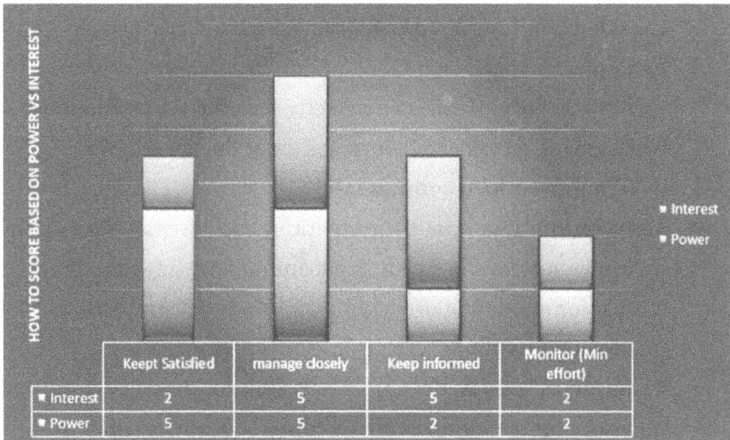

HOW TO SCORE BASED ON POWER VS INTEREST	Keept Satisfied	manage closely	Keep informed	Monitor (Min effort)
■ Interest	2	5	5	2
■ Power	5	5	2	2

Figure 2.24 Scoring methodology based on power versus interest

Other factors that can be used to judge engagement can be knowledge and rights.

2.2.6.3 Conflict Management

Conflict management[9] involves handling conflicts[24] or disagreements in a way that leads to a resolution. There are various approaches to conflict resolution, and one way to categorize them is through the "Win-Win,"

"Win-Lose," "Lose-Win," and "Lose-Lose" combinations. Here's a break-down of each:

1. **Win-Win (Collaboration/Problem-Solving)**
   - **Description:** In a Win-Win situation, both parties work together to find a solution that satisfies the interests and needs of everyone involved. It is a cooperative approach that aims to maximize both parties' outcomes.
   - **Example:** Two team members have different ideas for approaching a project. Through open communication and compromise, they find a solution that incorporates the strengths of both approaches, leading to a more robust project plan.

2. **Win-Lose (Competition/Force and Direct approach)**
   - **Description:** In a Win-Lose scenario, one party prevails at the expense of the other. It is a competitive approach where the focus is on achieving one's own goals without much consideration for the other party's interests.
   - **Example:** In a negotiation for a promotion, one employee may aggressively pursue their own interests, securing the promotion while leaving the other employees without the opportunity.

3. **Lose-Win (Smooth/Accommodate)**
   - **Description:** In a Lose-Win situation, one party sacrifices their own interests or needs to accommodate the other. It is an accommodating or yielding approach that emphasizes maintaining harmony, even if it means personal loss.
   - **Example:** A team leader agrees to a decision that they don't fully support avoiding conflict within the team, sacrificing their own preferences for the sake of team unity.

4. **Lose-Lose (Avoidance or Compromise or Reconcile)**
   - **Description:** In a Lose-Lose scenario, neither party achieves its full goals, and both may experience some level of loss. It can occur when conflicts are ignored or when a compromise is reached, but neither party is fully satisfied.
   - **Example:** Two business partners with different visions for the company might compromise on a middle-ground strategy. However, both may feel dissatisfied, resulting in a lose-lose outcome.

In a fictional case, sourced from Harvard Business Review,[12] a sports apparel manufacturer's CEO grapples with a conflict between the head of sales and the CFO, which is causing turmoil throughout the organization. The CEO, known for avoiding conflict, considers various options such as changing compensation schemes, termination, coaching, and team-building activities to address the situation. The case can have the following outcomes. **Win-Win:** The CEO aims to find solutions that satisfy both conflicting executives, fostering cooperation and alignment with company goals. *(Best Preferred is negotiation and problem-solving to achieve mutually beneficial outcomes.)* **Win-Lose:** Unilateral actions by the CEO, like firing one executive, may temporarily resolve conflict but breed resentment and disengagement. *(Tip: One should warn against such approaches, stressing the importance of preserving relationships for long-term success.)* **Lose-Win:** Ignoring the conflict to maintain harmony may seem like a solution but fails to address underlying issues. *(Tip: One should advocate for proactive conflict resolution to prevent lingering discontent.)* **Lose-Lose:** If conflict escalates unchecked, both parties suffer, leading to a toxic work environment and decreased performance. *(Tip: One should underscore the need for effective intervention and communication to prevent such scenarios and promote organizational well-being.)*

Hence, choosing the appropriate conflict resolution strategy depends on the context, the nature of the conflict, and the relationships involved. **Collaboration (Win-Win) is often seen as the ideal approach when building long-term relationships, while other strategies may be suitable depending on the situation and the goals of the parties involved.[20]**

2.2.7 Plan Communication

Plan Communications Management: This process involves defining the approach and plan for communication throughout the project. It establishes guidelines for information distribution, communication methods, frequency, and stakeholders' expectations. The goal is to ensure effective and efficient communication that supports project success.[9]

2.2.7.1 Inputs[20]

- **Project Management Plan**
  - The overall project management plan provides a foundation for the communication plan, as it includes various subsidiary plans and baselines.

- **Project Charter**
  - ° Understanding the project charter helps in identifying key stakeholders and their communication needs.
- **Stakeholder Register**
  - ° This document provides details about stakeholders, their communication needs, and their influence on the project.
- **Enterprise Environmental Factors**
  - ° External factors such as culture, infrastructure, and industry standards may influence communication planning.
- **Organizational Process Assets**
  - ° Historical information, templates, and lessons learned that can guide the communication planning process.

2.2.7.2 Tools and Techniques[9]

- **Expert Judgment**
  - ° Input from individuals with expertise in communication planning.
- **Data Gathering**
  - ° Methods like surveys and questionnaires to collect information on stakeholder communication needs.
- **Interpersonal and Team Skills**
  - ° Skills such as negotiation, influencing, and active listening to understand and address communication requirements.
- **Meetings**
  - ° Collaborative sessions to discuss communication planning with relevant stakeholders.
- **Communication Requirement Analysis**
  - ° Communication Requirement Analysis involves determining the information needs of project stakeholders. It aims to identify what information is needed, who needs it when they need it, and in what format.

Key Activities.[21] Identifying Stakeholders->Determining Information Needs->Defining Communication Methods->Establishing Communication Frequencies.

Communication Models.[20] Communication Models are theoretical frameworks that describe how communication processes work. These models help us understand the dynamics of sending and receiving messages.

1. Linear Communication Model: Involves a sender transmitting a message through a channel to a receiver. This basic model includes elements like encoding, message, channel, decoding, and feedback.
2. Transactional Communication Model: Emphasizes communication as a continuous, two-way process where both parties (sender and receiver) play active roles. It recognizes that communication is ongoing and that feedback is crucial for mutual understanding.
3. Interactive Communication Model: Similar to the transactional model, this model involves a continuous exchange of information, feedback, and adjustment. It recognizes the dynamic nature of communication in complex environments.
4. Berlo's SMCR Model: Focuses on Source, Message, Channel, and Receiver. It adds the element of the context in which communication occurs, recognizing that various factors influence the effectiveness of communication.
5. Shannon-Weaver Model: Involves a sender encoding a message, transmitting it through a channel, and the receiver decoding the message. It introduces the concept of noise, which can interfere with the transmission of the message.

Communication Methods.[20] Communication Methods are the various ways information is exchanged within a project team and with stakeholders.

These methods will prepare you for preference-based mindset questions in PMP.

1. Meetings: **Face-to-face** (best preferred) or virtual gatherings for discussions, decision making, and information sharing.
2. Reports and Dashboards: Providing **regular updates** and summaries of project progress and key metrics. *Example methods like Fishbowl may be critical for DOD-related projects where minute info needs to be tracked.*

3. Presentations: Using slideshows or verbal communication to convey information to a group **(methods of training).**

4. E-mails and Memos: Written communication for formal announcements, updates, or documentation.

5. Workshops and Training Sessions: Interactive skills-building sessions or addressing specific project needs.

Selection Criteria: The choice of communication methods depends on factors like the nature of information, audience preferences, and the urgency of communication (for example, a page to all instead of calling for a meeting when something needs urgency can serve better).

2.2.7.3 Outputs

- Communications Management Plan:[20]
  - The primary output detailing the communication needs of stakeholders, methods, frequency, and escalation procedures.
- Project Documents Updates:
  - Updates to documents like stakeholder register based on communication planning.
- Enterprise Environmental Factors Updates:
  - Updates to factors such as organizational culture or infrastructure that may affect communication.
- Organizational Process Assets Updates:
  - Updates to communication templates and lessons learned for future projects.

The "Plan Communications Management" process sets the foundation for effective communication throughout the project life cycle, ensuring that information is distributed promptly and appropriately to meet stakeholder needs and expectations.

2.2.8 Plan Risk

In Project Management,[20] risks can be categorized into several types based on various criteria. Here are some common types of risks:

Table 2.9 Types of risks

Category	Description	Examples
Strategic	Risks related to overall organizational goals and objectives	Changes in market conditions, competition, technology advancements
Operational	Risks associated with day-to-day activities and processes	Process failures, human errors, system breakdowns
Financial	Risks related to financial activities and resources	Budget overruns, cost estimation errors, currency fluctuations
Compliance	**Risks associated with legal and regulatory requirements**	**Noncompliance with laws, regulations, ethical standards, Usually whenever there are risks like this, and it's confirmed to have these risks, PM should first refer to the organizational guidelines**
Project-Specific	Risks specific to the project, including scope, schedule, cost, quality	Scope creep, schedule delays, resource limitations, technical challenges
Technical	Risks related to technology, equipment, tools, and technical processes	Software defects, hardware failures, compatibility issues
Market	Risks related to changes in market conditions, demand, competition	Market fluctuations, competitor actions, shifts in consumer preferences
Environmental	Risks associated with natural disasters, climate change, and other environmental factors	Weather disruptions, resource scarcity, environmental regulations
Human Resource	Risks related to the workforce, including skills, turnover, morale	Skill gaps, employee dissatisfaction, labor disputes
Legal	Risks related to legal actions, lawsuits, and disputes	Contractual disputes, intellectual property infringement, regulatory violations
Supply Chain	Risks associated with disruptions in the supply chain	Supplier issues, logistical challenges, transportation delays
Reputation	Risks related to the organization's reputation and public perception	Negative publicity, product recalls, ethical scandals
Cybersecurity	Risks related to information security and data breaches	Cyberattacks, malware infections, unauthorized access
Health and Safety	**Risks related to the well-being of individuals involved in the project**	**Accidents, occupational hazards, health-related issues, Usually whenever there are risks like this, and it's confirmed to have these risks, projects should be stopped immediately.**

2.2.8.1 Inputs, Outputs, Tools, and Techniques

Table 2.10 ITTO—Project lifecycle: Planning risk[9]

Process	Inputs	Tools and Techniques	Outputs
Plan Risk Management	Project Management Plan, Project Charter, Environmental Factors, Organizational Assets	Expert Judgment, Data Gathering, Meetings	Risk Management Plan
Identify Risks	Project Management Plan, Project Documents, Procurement Documentation, Environmental Factors, Organizational Assets	Expert Judgment, Data Gathering, Brainstorming, Meetings	Risk Register, Risk Report, Project Document Updates
Perform Qualitative Risk Analysis	Project Management Plan, Project Documents, Environmental Factors, Organizational Assets	Expert Judgment, Data Gathering, Data Analysis, Risk Categorization, Probability and Impact Assessment, Meetings	Risk Register Updates, Risk Report, Project Document Updates
Perform Quantitative Risk Analysis	Risk Management Plan, Risk Register, Project Documents, Environmental Factors, Organizational Assets	Data Gathering, Sensitivity Analysis, Quantitative Modeling, Expert Judgment	Risk Register Updates, Risk Report
Plan Risk Responses	Risk Management Plan, Risk Register, Project Documents, Environmental Factors, Organizational Assets	Risk Response Strategies, Team and Interpersonal Skills, Expert Judgment	Risk Register Updates, Change Requests, Project Management Plan Updates, Project Document Updates

2.2.8.2 Risk versus Issue

In project management, risks and issues are distinct concepts that refer to different aspects of potential challenges. **Risk** is an uncertain event or condition that, if it occurs, may positively or negatively impact the project's objectives. Risks are events that have not happened yet but may occur in the future.

Key Points

- Risks are *future-oriented* and may or may not happen.
  {keywords you are looking for are could, might, may}
- They are uncertain events that can affect project objectives.
- Risk management involves identifying, assessing, and responding to potential risks.

Example

- **Risk:** There is a risk that the key supplier *may* face delays in delivering critical components due to unforeseen circumstances like natural disasters or production issues.

Whereas issue[20] is a current problem or challenge that has already occurred and is affecting the project. Issues need to be addressed to prevent negative impacts on the project's progress.

Table 2.11 Key differences issue versus risk

Aspect	Issue	Risk
Timing	Current problem, already happened	Future event, may or may not occur
Nature	Known problem, currently affecting project	Uncertain event, potential positive or negative impact
Management Approach	Resolution and corrective actions	Identification, assessment, and response planning
Focus	Addressing existing problems	Preventing potential problems

Table 2.12 Example

Scenario	Issue	Risk
Software defect discovered during testing	Delay in project schedule due to code revision and retesting	Risk of software defects during development
Team member resignation	Resource gap requiring immediate resolution	Risk of losing key term members

Logs capturing Risks are Risk logs, and logs capturing Issues are known as Issue logs.

2.2.8.3 Risk management Plan versus Risk register

Table 2.13 Risk management plan versus risk register[9]

Aspect	Risk Management Plan	Risk Register
Purpose	Guides overall risk management activities	Captures details about identified risks and their status
Scope	Encompasses the entire project	Focuses on specific risks identified during the project
Content	Outlines approach, methodologies, and responsibilities	Contains specific details about individual risks
Development	Developed early in the project planning phase	Created and continuously updated throughout the project
Role in Risk Management	Provides strategic direction for risk management	Serves as an operational tool for tracking and managing risks
Updates	May be updated as needed during the project	Continuously updated as new risks are identified and managed

2.2.8.4 Risk Breakdown Structure

A Risk Breakdown Structure[9] (RBS) is a hierarchical decomposition of risks, systematically categorizing and understanding potential risks within a project.

Here's an example of a simplified Risk Breakdown Structure for a software development project, along with some sample risks:

Table 2.14 Risk breakdown structure

Category	Subcategory	Description	Probability	Impact	Risk Owner
Project Risks	1.1 Lack of Stakeholder Involvement	Stakeholders may not be actively engaged, leading to misunderstandings and changes.	Medium	High	Project Manager

Table 2.14 (Continued)

Category	Subcategory	Description	Probability	Impact	Risk Owner
Project Risks	1.2 Unclear Project Objectives	Unclear objectives can lead to scope creep and rework.	Medium	High	Project Manager
Project Risks	1.3 Insufficient Project Budget	Budget constraints can limit resources and impact project goals.	Low	Medium	Project Manager
Technical Risks	2.1 Compatibility Issues with Legacy Systems	Integrating with existing systems may pose challenges and delays.	High	Moderate	Technical Lead
Technical Risks	2.2 Software Integration Challenges	Third-party software integration may lead to development delays.	High	Moderate	Technical Lead
Technical Risks	2.3 Technology Obsolescence	Rapid technological advancements may render project technology outdated.	Low	Medium	Technical Lead
Resource Risks	3.1 Key Team Member Attrition	Loss of key personnel can affect knowledge continuity and progress.	Low	Major	Project Manager
Resource Risks	3.2 Insufficient Skill Set of Team Members	Team members may lack necessary skills, impacting project quality.	Medium	Medium	Project Manager
Resource Risks	3.3 Limited Availability of Testing Environments	Lack of testing environments can delay testing and bug identification.	Medium	Low	Project Manager
External Risks	4.1 Vendor Delivery Delays	Delays from vendors can impact project schedules and deliverables.	Medium	High	Procurement Manager

(Continued)

Table 2.14 (Continued)

Category	Subcategory	Description	Probability	Impact	Risk Owner
External Risks	4.2 Changes in Regulatory Requirements	Regulatory changes may require project adjustments and rework.	Low	High	Project Manager
External Risks	4.3 Economic Downturn	Economic downturns may impact project funding and resource availability.	Medium	High	Project Sponsor
Quality Risks	5.1 Insufficient Testing Coverage	Inadequate testing may lead to undetected defects and rework.	High	High	Quality Assurance Lead
Quality Risks	5.2 Inadequate Code Review Process	Insufficient code review can introduce errors and security vulnerabilities.	Medium	High	Development Lead
Quality Risks	5.3 Scope Creep	Continuous changes to project scope can lead to increased development time and resource constraints.	High	Major	Product Owner

This example illustrates how risks can be categorized within a Risk Breakdown Structure, providing a structured approach to identifying and managing risks throughout the project lifecycle. Each risk is associated with a specific category, making prioritizing and addressing potential challenges easier.

2.2.8.5 Some Widely Used Risk Management Tools

Risk management tools are essential for identifying, analyzing, and mitigating risks in a project or organizational context. Here are some common types of risk management tools: *These tools are important from an exam perspective.*

Table 2.15 Risk management tools[9]

Tool	Description	Benefits
Risk Register	Comprehensive log of identified risks, their details, and planned responses.	Centralized tracking and management of risks.
Risk Matrix	Graphical representation of risk probability and impact for prioritization.	Helps determine appropriate response levels.
SWOT Analysis	Identifies internal and external factors (Strengths, Weaknesses, Opportunities, Threats) impacting project objectives.	Provides a holistic view of potential influences.
Decision Trees	Graphical representation of decisions and their consequences.	Facilitates evaluation of alternative courses of action and associated risks.
Cause and Effect Diagram	Identifies potential causes of a specific problem or risk.	Helps understand root causes and contributing factors.
Checklists	Lists potential risks or risk factors for systematic review.	Ensures comprehensive identification of potential risks.
Risk Heat Maps	Visual representation of risk severity using color coding.	Provides quick understanding of risk distribution.
Monte Carlo Simulation	Quantitative tool modeling the impact of different risk scenarios.	Offers a range of possible project outcomes based on probability distributions.
Risk Modeling Software	Specialized software for creating and analyzing risk models.	Supports quantitative analysis and scenario testing.
Risk Assessment Questionnaires and Surveys	Tools to gather input from stakeholders for risk assessment and prioritization.	Facilitates collaborative risk identification and evaluation.
Scenario Analysis	Evaluates different potential future scenarios and their associated risks.	Helps prepare for various possible outcomes.
Dependency Analysis	Identifies dependencies between project tasks and components.	Crucial for anticipating risks associated with interconnected elements.
Historical Information and Lessons Learned Databases	Access to historical data from past projects for identifying recurring risks and lessons learned.	Informs risk planning and response strategies.
Expert Judgment	Seeking input from subject matter experts for risk identification, assessment, and response.	Valuable qualitative tool for informed decision making.
Risk Dashboard	Visual representation of key risk indicators and their current status.	Provides a quick overview of the risk landscape.

Other miscellaneous risk-related terminologies.[9]

1. **Risk Appetite:** The degree of uncertainty an organization or individual is willing to accept in anticipation of a reward. It influences the approach to risk-taking within a project.

2. **Risk Tolerance:** The degree, amount, or volume of risk an organization or individual will withstand. It is often associated with specific objectives and can vary across different risk categories.

3. **Secondary Risks:** Risks that arise directly from implementing risk response strategies. These are risks introduced while trying to mitigate or eliminate primary risks.

4. **Workarounds:** Unplanned responses to deal with risks that were not identified or for which a response was not planned. Workarounds are implemented when a risk occurs without a predefined response.

5. **Fallback Plans:** Predefined actions to be taken if the primary response to a risk is ineffective. Fallback plans are developed as a contingency in case the initial risk response does not work as expected.

6. **Contingency Reserves:** Additional time, budget, or resources set aside to address identified risks that may occur. Contingency reserves are part of the project baseline.

7. **Residual Risks:** Risks that remain after risk response planning and execution. Residual risks are the risks that are not completely eliminated or transferred.

8. **Risk Urgency Assessment:** An evaluation of the timing of the risk responses. It helps determine when the risk response strategies should be implemented to be most effective.

9. **Variance and Trend Analysis:** Monitoring the project's performance against the project management plan. Variance and trend analysis can help identify potential risks based on deviations from the planned performance.

10. **Technical Performance Measurement (TPM):** Metrics used to assess the technical performance of the project work. TPM can reveal risks related to technical aspects of the project.

11. **Risk Data Quality Assessment:** Evaluating the accuracy and reliability of risk-related data. It ensures that the data used for risk analysis is of high quality.

12. **Risk Reviews:** Periodic assessments of the effectiveness of risk responses and the risk management process. Risk reviews help identify emerging risks and assess the performance of risk response strategies.

2.2.8.6 Failure Mode Effect Analysis, Decision Tree analysis, Probability, and Impact Analysis

Example of FMEA (Failure Mode and Effects Analysis[9])

Scenario: Let's consider a manufacturing process for producing electronic components. One critical step in the process is soldering components onto a circuit board.

Steps in FMEA

1. Identify Failure Modes
   - **Failure Mode 1:** Insufficient soldering
   - **Failure Mode 2:** Excessive soldering
2. **Identify Effects of Failure**
   - **Effect 1:** Insufficient soldering can lead to poor electrical connections and component failure.
   - **Effect 2:** Excessive soldering can cause short circuits and damage components.
3. **Assign Severity, Occurrence, and Detection Ratings (Scale 1–10)**

Table 2.16 FMEA table

Failure Mode/ Effect	Severity (S)	Occurrence (O)	Detection (D)
Insufficient Soldering (FM1/Effect 1)	9	5	8
Excessive Soldering (FM2/Effect 2)	8	4	7

4. **Calculate Risk Priority Number (RPN)**
   - RPN = Severity × Occurrence × Detection

Table 2.17 FMEA table values

Failure Mode/Effect	RPN
Insufficient Soldering (FM1/Effect 1)	$9 \times 5 \times 8 = 360$
Excessive Soldering (FM2/Effect 2)	$8 \times 4 \times 7 = 224$

5. **Prioritize Actions**
   - Prioritize actions based on the RPN values. For example, focus on reducing the RPN of the higher priority failure mode.
6. **Implement Improvements**
   - Implement process changes or controls to reduce the likelihood or severity of identified failure modes.

Example of Decision Tree Analysis

Scenario: Consider a project manager deciding on a project approach for software development.

Decision Tree Analysis

1. **Decision Node**
   - **Decision:** Choose between two project approaches: Agile or Waterfall.
2. **Chance Nodes (Probability of Success/Failure for Each Approach)**
   - **Chance Node 1:** Probability of Agile Success = 0.8
   - **Chance Node 2:** Probability of Agile Failure = 1 – Probability of Agile Success = 0.2
   - **Chance Node 3:** Probability of Waterfall Success = 0.6
   - **Chance Node 4:** Probability of Waterfall Failure = 1 – Probability of Waterfall Success = 0.4
3. **Terminal Nodes (Outcomes)**
   - **Outcome Node 1:** Agile Success -> High Profit = $100,000
   - **Outcome Node 2:** Agile Failure -> Moderate Profit = $50,000
   - **Outcome Node 3:** Waterfall Success -> Moderate Profit = $60,000

- **Outcome Node 4:** Waterfall Failure -> Low Profit = $30,000

4. **Calculate Expected Monetary Value (EMV) for Each Decision**
   - EMV = (Probability of Outcome 1 × Value of Outcome 1) + (Probability of Outcome 2 × Value of Outcome 2)

Table 2.18 EMV calculations

Decision Node	EMV
Agile Decision	(0.8 × $100,000) + (0.2 × $50,000) = $90,000
Waterfall Decision	(0.6 × $60,000) + (0.4 × $30,000) = $48,000

5. **Make Decision**
   - Choose the decision with the highest EMV. In this case, the Agile approach is preferred due to its higher expected monetary value.

     Decision Tree Analysis helps project managers make decisions by considering different scenarios and their associated probabilities, leading to an informed choice based on expected outcomes.

Example of Probability versus Impact Analysis

Scenario: The software development project involves creating a new feature requiring third-party API integration.

Table 2.19 Example of probability versus impact analysis

Identify Risk	Recognize potential threats to the project.	Third-party API downtime during integration
Assess Probability	Estimate the likelihood of the risk occurring.	High (4 on a scale of 1–5)
Assess Impact	Evaluate the potential consequences of the risk.	Moderate (3 on a scale of 1–5)
Calculate Risk Severity	Multiply probability and impact to determine overall risk level.	12 (4 x 3)
Interpret Severity	Analyze the risk level based on the calculated value.	Moderate—requires attention and response

(Continued)

Table 2.19 (Continued)

Determine Risk Response	Develop strategies to address the identified risk.	Implement alternative API integration methods, establish contingency plans, and create communication strategies.
Monitor and Update	Continuously track the risk and update assessments as needed.	Monitor changes in probability and impact throughout the project.

2.2.8.7 Threat versus Opportunity

In the context of risk management, organizations or project teams can adopt different types of responses or strategies to address identified risks. These strategies are often categorized based on how the organization chooses to deal with the risk. Here are the common risk types concerning risk responses: A positive Risk is called an **Opportunity**, and a negative risk is a **Threat.**

A project manager can implement the following strategies for threats.

Table 2.20 Strategies for Threats

Strategy	Definition	Example
Avoidance	Eliminate the threat or prevent the risk from occurring.	Choosing alternative technology due to high failure probability.
Acceptance	Acknowledge the risk and bear the consequences if it materializes.	Accepting potential weather delays for an outdoor event with minimal impact.
Mitigation	Reduce the probability or impact of the risk.	Implementing agile development to accommodate potential requirement changes.
Transfer	Shift the risk to another party through insurance, contracts, or outsourcing.	Purchasing insurance coverage for financial losses due to natural disasters.
Escalation	Raise the issue to a higher level of management for guidance or decision making.	Escalating compliance-related risks to the legal department or senior management.

It's important to note that these risk responses are not mutually exclusive, and a combination of strategies may be used to address a particular risk. The selection of a specific risk response depends on factors such as the nature of the risk, its impact on project objectives, and the organization's risk tolerance.

In addition to the traditional risk responses, specific responses are associated with opportunities. Here are the common types of **opportunity responses** in the context of risk management:

Table 2.21 Strategies for Opportunities

Strategy	Definition	Example
Exploit	Maximize the potential benefits of an opportunity.	Allocate additional resources to expedite development and gain a competitive advantage.
Enhance	Increase the probability and/or positive impact of an opportunity.	Invest in additional promotional activities to maximize the impact of a collaboration.
Accept	Acknowledge the opportunity without further action if it aligns with objectives.	Accept cost savings in materials due to a favorable market condition.
Share	Collaborate with external parties to leverage their capabilities and resources.	Partner with a research institution to bring innovative products to market faster.
Escalate	Raise awareness of the opportunity to higher levels of management for support or decisions.	Escalate a new market opportunity to senior management for resource allocation and strategic approval.

2.2.9 Plan Procurement

Table 2.22 ITTO—Project lifecycle: Planning Procurement[21]

Inputs	Tools and Techniques	Outputs
Project Management Plan	Expert Judgment	Procurement Management Plan, Procurement strategy, Bid Documents
Project Documents	Market Research	Procurement Statement of Work (SOW)
Enterprise Environmental Factors (EEFs)	Meetings	Source Selection Criteria
Organizational Process Assets (OPAs)	Data gathering, Data analysis, Source Selection analysis	Make-or-Buy Decisions
Business Documents		Independent cost estimates, OPA updates, Project document updates, Change Requests

Let's revisit some key terms here. *Note that these are important from an exam perspective.*

Table 2.23a Procurement management terminology and tools summary table

Term	Description	Example
Procurement Management Plan	Outlines how procurement processes will be managed throughout the project	Specifies contract types, risk management approaches, and monitoring/control methods
Procurement Strategy	Defines the overall approach to acquiring goods or services	Decides on competitive bidding, negotiation, or partnerships
Bid Documents	Information provided to potential suppliers about the project, specifications, terms, and conditions	Software development project details requirements, timeline, and evaluation criteria
Request for Information (RFI)	Gathers information from potential suppliers about their products, services, or capabilities	Used before construction projects to gather information about materials, methods, and suppliers
Request for Proposal (RFP)	Detailed document outlining project requirements, scope of work, and evaluation criteria	Software development project details specifications, timeline, and criteria, inviting vendor proposals
Request for Quotation (RFQ)	Requests quotes from suppliers for specific products or services	Used for straightforward procurements with well-defined specifications, e.g., office furniture
Bid Conference (Pre-bid Meeting)	Gathering for potential suppliers to seek clarification on project requirements and address concerns	Construction project conference allows contractors to ask questions about scope, specifications, and bidding

Table 2.23b Procurement management terminology and tools summary table

Term	Description	Example
Bid Opening	Process of opening and reviewing submitted bids, typically done publicly	Public infrastructure project opens bids from construction companies in the presence of representatives.
Bid Bond	Guarantee provided by a bidder to ensure they accept the contract and provide required performance/payment bonds	Construction company includes a bid bond with its government project bid.
Bidders Conference	Similar to bid conference, provides an opportunity for potential bidders to learn more about the project	Government agency hosting a bidder's conference for a complex procurement

Table 2.23b (Continued)

Term	Description	Example
Responsive Bid	A bid that meets all requirements and criteria specified in the solicitation documents	Only bids meeting technical and financial criteria are considered responsive in competitive bidding.
Unsolicited Proposal	A proposal submitted by a vendor without a specific request from the buyer	A technology company submits an unsolicited proposal to a government agency suggesting a new software solution.
Procurement Statement of Work (SOW)	Clearly defines the work to be performed, including specifications, deliverables, and acceptance criteria	Construction project SOW specifies building requirements, materials, design specifications, and completion deadlines.
Source Selection Criteria	Outline the factors used to evaluate and select suppliers, including cost, expertise, past performance, and so on	Software development project prioritizes vendors with relevant experience and competitive pricing.
Make-or-Buy Decisions	Determine whether to perform an activity in-house or procure it externally, considering expertise, cost, and strategic importance	Electronics company makes circuit boards in-house but buys standard office furniture.
Independent Cost Estimates	Assessments conducted by external experts to determine the expected cost of goods or services	Independent cost estimator evaluates expected costs for materials, labor, and equipment in a construction project.

Table 2.23c Procurement management terminology and tools summary table

Term	Description	Example
OPA Updates	Revise organizational documents based on procurement experiences	Updating templates, lessons learned repository, and project documents after completing a procurement process
Project Document Updates	Reflect changes in project documents influenced by procurement activities	Updating project documents after completing a procurement process
Change Requests	Submitted if modifications to procurement processes or documents are needed	Submitting a change request if modifications to project documents influenced by procurement are needed

After completing a procurement process, the organization updates its templates, lessons learned repository, and project documents to incorporate insights gained from the procurement.

2.2.9.1 Flow Chart of the Procurement Process

Identify Need & Define Requirements
↓
Prepare Procurement Plan
↓
Conduct Market Research
↓
Develop Procurement Strategy
↓
Obtain Internal Approvals
↓
Create Solicitation Documents
↓
Publish Solicitation
↓
Conduct Bid Conferences
↓
Receive and Review Bids/Proposals
↓
Evaluate Bids/Proposals
↓
Negotiate Terms
↓
Select Supplier
↓
Award Contract/Purchase Order
↓
Notify Unsuccessful Bidders
↓
Establish Contract Management Plan
↓
Monitor Performance
↓
Receive Deliverables/Services
↓
Verify and Approve Invoices
↓
Closeout Contract
↓
Conduct Procurement Audits
↓
End

Figure 2.25 Flowchart of the procurement process

2.2.9.2 Types of Contracts

1. Fixed-Price[20] Contract (Lump Sum or Firm Fixed Price)
- **Description:** A contract where the buyer pays a predetermined, fixed amount for the services or goods, regardless of the actual costs incurred by the seller.
- **When to Use:** Suitable for well-defined projects with minimal uncertainties, where the scope and requirements are clear.

Table 2.24 Types of fixed price contracts

Contract Type	Description	Example
Firm Fixed-Price (FFP) Contract	The buyer pays a fixed amount, and the seller is responsible for all costs, whether they are higher or lower than initially estimated.	A construction project where a contractor agrees to build a facility for a fixed price, covering labor, materials, and overhead costs
Fixed-Price Incentive Fee (FPIF) Contract	The buyer pays a fixed price, and an additional incentive fee is provided to the seller based on performance metrics, such as cost savings or schedule acceleration.	A software development project where the contractor receives a fixed price plus an incentive fee for delivering the product ahead of schedule
Fixed-Price with Economic Price Adjustment (FP-EPA) Contract	The fixed price can be adjusted based on predefined economic factors such as inflation, allowing for changes in market conditions.	A long-term contract for the supply of raw materials where the price is adjusted annually based on changes in market prices

2. Cost-Reimbursable[20] Contract:
- **Description:** The buyer reimburses the seller for the allowable or agreed-upon costs, and the seller also receives additional payment for profit.
- **When to Use:** Appropriate when the scope is not well-defined, and flexibility is needed to accommodate changes during the project.

Table 2.25 Types of cost-reimbursable contracts

Contract Type	Description	Example
Cost-Plus-Fixed-Fee (CPFF) Contract	The buyer reimburses the seller for allowable costs, and a fixed fee (profit) is paid as a lump sum or a percentage of the estimated costs.	A research and development project where a contractor is reimbursed for incurred costs, and a fixed fee is added to cover profit
Cost-Plus-Incentive-Fee (CPIF) Contract	The buyer reimburses allowable costs, and the seller receives an additional incentive fee based on meeting or exceeding specified performance criteria.	A construction project where the contractor is reimbursed for costs and receives an incentive fee for completing the project ahead of schedule
Cost-Plus-Award-Fee (CPAF) Contract	The buyer reimburses allowable costs, and an award fee is provided based on the buyer's assessment of the seller's performance against predetermined criteria.	A government contract for consulting services where the contractor is reimbursed for costs, and an award fee is determined based on performance evaluations
Cost-Plus-Percentage-of-Cost (CPPC) Contract	The buyer reimburses the seller for allowable costs, and the seller receives a percentage of the total costs as profit.	A software development project where the contractor is reimbursed for incurred costs, and the profit is a specified percentage of the total costs

3. **Time and Materials (T&M)[20] Contract:**
   - **Description:** Payment is based on the time spent on the project and the materials used, often with an hourly rate for labor and direct costs for materials.
   - **When to Use:** Suitable for projects where the scope is not well-defined, and flexibility is needed, but with more control than a cost-reimbursable contract.

Table 2.26 Other types of contracts

Contract Type	Description	When to Use
Unit Price Contract	The buyer pays a fixed price for each unit of work or service delivered by the seller.	Appropriate when the quantity of work is uncertain, and payment is based on measurable units.
Time and Materials with a Cap (T&M with Cap)	Similar to a time and materials contract, but with a maximum limit (cap) on the total amount payable by the buyer.	Suitable when flexibility is needed, but the buyer wants to limit the overall project cost.

Table 2.26 (Continued)

Contract Type	Description	When to Use
Joint Venture Agreement	An agreement between two or more parties to collaborate on a specific project or business activity, sharing risks, resources, and profits.	Appropriate when parties want to combine their strengths for a specific project or business opportunity.
Partnership Agreement	An agreement between two or more parties to operate a business and share in its profits and losses.	Suitable for long-term business relationships where parties want to share responsibilities and outcomes.
Non-Disclosure Agreement (NDA)	An agreement to protect confidential information and prevent its unauthorized disclosure.	Essential when sharing sensitive information during negotiations, collaborations, or partnerships.
Service Level Agreement (SLA)	A contract that defines the level of service a provider is expected to deliver and the metrics by which that service will be measured.	Common in service-oriented industries to ensure agreed-upon service standards.
Employment Contract	Outlines the terms and conditions of employment, including roles, responsibilities, compensation, and termination clauses.	Essential for formalizing the relationship between an employer and an employee.
Consulting Agreement	An agreement between a consultant and a client, outlining the scope of work, deliverables, compensation, and other terms.	Used when hiring external expertise for a specific project or advisory services.
Memorandum of Understanding (MOU) or Letter of Intent (LOI)	A preliminary agreement outlining the general terms and conditions of a potential transaction or collaboration.	Often used at the initial stages of negotiations to express mutual interest and intention.
Purchase Order (PO)	A document issued by a buyer to a seller, indicating the types, quantities, and agreed prices for products or services.	Common for simple, routine transactions with established suppliers.
License Agreement	Grants permission to use, sell, or distribute a product or intellectual property under specified conditions.	Used when allowing others to use or commercialize intellectual property, software, or products.
Franchise Agreement	An agreement that grants an individual or entity the right to operate a business using the franchisor's brand and business model.	Used when expanding a successful business model to new locations.

2.2.10 Plan Stakeholders

Inputs: Project Charter,[2] Project Management Plan, Project Documents,[13] Agreements, EEF, OPA

Tools and Techniques: Expert Judgment, Data Gathering, Data Analysis, Decision Making, Data Representation, Meetings.

Outputs: Stakeholder engagement plan

2.2.10.1 NPS (Net Promoter Score)

Net Promoter Score[20] (NPS) is a metric used to measure customer loyalty and satisfaction. It is often employed in stakeholder analysis to gauge the likelihood of stakeholders recommending a product, a service, or, in a broader sense, a project. The NPS is based on a simple question: "On a scale of 0 to 10, how likely are you to recommend [product/project/service] to others?" Respondents are categorized into three groups:

Table 2.27 Score category: NPS

Stakeholder Category	Score Range	Description
Promoters	9–10	Highly satisfied stakeholders who are likely to actively promote the project to others
Passives	7–8	Stakeholders who are satisfied but not particularly enthusiastic. They are neutral and may not actively promote or criticize the project
Detractors	0–6	Dissatisfied stakeholders who may spread negative feedback about the project

The **NPS** is determined by taking the percentage of promoters and subtracting the percentage of detractors. The resulting score provides an overall measure of stakeholder satisfaction and the likelihood of project success.

2.2.10.2 Prioritization Schema

A prioritization schema[20] is a systematic approach to organizing and ranking stakeholders based on their importance, influence, or impact on a project. Different stakeholders have varying degrees of interest and power, and a prioritization schema helps identify key stakeholders who can significantly affect or be affected by the project.

The schema may involve categorizing stakeholders into groups such as:

Figure 2.26 Schema categorizing stakeholders into groups

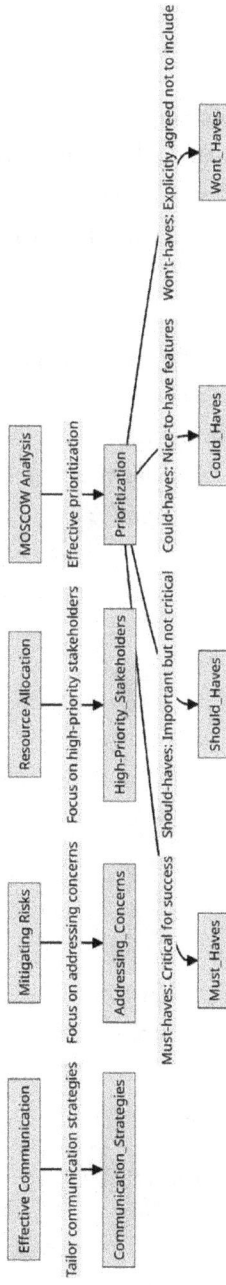

Figure 2.27 Schema for stakeholder analysis

Tip: How They Help in Stakeholder Analysis is important for mind-set-based questions in PMP.

Example

Consider a software development project. Must-haves might include core functionalities like user authentication and data storage. Should-haves could be additional features like real-time notifications and could-haves might include features that enhance the user experience but aren't critical. Won't-haves might involve features that are deemed unnecessary for the current version but could be considered for future releases.

MoSCoW provides a structured approach to prioritize requirements, ensuring that project teams focus on delivering the most impactful features within given constraints.

Tip: Let's try some questions to check the basics for the PMP examination. These will help prepare the mindset as well.

2.2.11 Question and Answer Based on "Stage-Planning"

2.2.11.1 Section I

One-Word Question

1. Define integration in project management.

Keyword Questions

2. What is the fundamental purpose served by the Project Management Plan in project integration?
3. Name a specific tool or technique employed in the initiation phase during the Develop Project Charter process.
4. Elaborate on the role and significance of the Change Control Board (CCB) within project integration.

Multiple-Choice Questions (MCQs)

5. Which document is primarily produced as an output of the Develop Project Charter process?
a. Project Scope Statement b. Project Management Plan c. Project Charter d. Project Stakeholder Register

6. Identify the process responsible for confirming project or phase completion, obtaining deliverable acceptance, and archiving project information.

   a. Direct and Manage Project Work b. Monitor and Control Project Work c. Validate Scope d. Close Project or Phase

7. In the context of project integration, what is the key function of the Project Management Information System (PMIS)?

   a. Develop project schedule b. Document lessons learned c. Facilitate communication and collaboration d. Control project scope.

Mix and Match Question

8. Connect the following project management processes with their corresponding descriptions:

   A. Direct and Manage Project Work B. Develop Project Management Plan C. Monitor and Control Project Work D. Close Project or Phase

   ○ Executing the work defined in the project management plan
   ○ Finalizing all activities across all process groups
   ○ Defining, preparing, and coordinating all subsidiary plans
   ○ Tracking, reviewing, and reporting project performance

Match Question

9. Match the following terms with their corresponding descriptions:

   A. _____ Project Charter B. _____ Project Manager C. _____ Change Control Board (CCB) D. _____ Lessons Learned

   ○ Documented information that authorizes the project
   ○ Individual responsible for achieving project objectives
   ○ Formal group responsible for approving or rejecting changes to the project
   ○ Knowledge gained from the project that can be applied to future projects

Fill in the Blank Questions

10. The Develop Project Management Plan process involves defining, preparing, and coordinating all subsidiary plans and integrating them into a comprehensive _____.

11. In the Close Project or Phase process, the project manager obtains final _____ from relevant stakeholders.

Multiple Options Correct Questions

12. Which components are typically included in the Project Management Plan? (Select all that apply.)

    a. Risk Management Plan b. Quality Management Plan c. Stakeholder Register d. Resource Histogram

13. Identify the processes falling under the Integration Management knowledge area. (Select all that apply.)

    a. Validate Scope b. Control Scope c. Develop Project Charter d. Develop Project Schedule

Answers

Table 2.28 Answers to section-1

Question Type	Question	Answer
One-Word	Define integration in project management.	Unification
Keyword	What is the fundamental purpose served by the Project Management Plan in project integration?	To guide project execution, monitor and control the project, and close the project.
Keyword	Name a specific tool or technique employed in the initiation phase during the Develop Project Charter process.	Expert judgment
Keyword	Elaborate on the role and significance of the Change Control Board (CCB) within project integration.	The Change Control Board (CCB) is a formal group responsible for approving or rejecting changes to the project. Its significance lies in ensuring that changes align with project objectives and do not negatively impact the project.
MCQ	Which document is primarily produced as an output of the Develop Project Charter process?	c. Project Charter

Table 2.28 (Continued)

Question Type	Question	Answer
MCQ	Identify the process responsible for confirming project or phase completion, obtaining deliverable acceptance, and archiving project information.	d. Close Project or Phase
MCQ	In the context of project integration, what is the key function of the Project Management Information System (PMIS)?	c. Facilitate communication and collaboration
Mix and Match	Connect the following project management processes with their corresponding descriptions:	
	* Executing the work defined in the project management plan.	A. Direct and Manage Project Work
	* Finalizing all activities across all process groups.	D. Close Project or Phase
	* Defining, preparing, and coordinating all subsidiary plans.	B. Develop Project Management Plan
	* Tracking, reviewing, and reporting project performance.	C. Monitor and Control Project Work
Match	Match the following terms with their corresponding descriptions:	
	* Documented information that authorizes the project.	A. Project Charter
	* Individual responsible for achieving project objectives.	B. Project Manager
	* Formal group responsible for approving or rejecting changes to the project.	C. Change Control Board (CCB)
	* Knowledge gained from the project that can be applied to future projects.	D. Lessons Learned
Fill in the Blank	The Develop Project Management Plan process involves defining, preparing, and coordinating all subsidiary plans and integrating them into a comprehensive _____.	Project management plan

(Continued)

Table 2.28 (Continued)

Question Type	Question	Answer
Fill in the Blank	In the Close Project or Phase process, the project manager obtains final _____ from relevant stakeholders.	Acceptance
Multiple Options Correct	Which components are typically included in the Project Management Plan? (Select all that apply)	
	* a. Risk Management Plan	
	* b. Quality Management Plan	
	c. Stakeholder Register	
	d. Resource Histogram	
Multiple Options Correct	Identify the processes falling under the Integration Management knowledge area. (Select all that apply)	(Not typically included)
	* a. Validate Scope	(Not under Integration Management)
	* b. Control Scope	(Not under Integration Management)
	* c. Develop Project Charter	
	* d. Develop Project Schedule	
Mix and Match	Connect the following terms related to project integration:	
	* Documented information that authorizes the project.	A. Project Charter
	* Individual responsible for achieving project objectives.	B. Project Manager
	* Formal group responsible for approving or rejecting changes to the project.	C. Change Control Board (CCB)
	* Knowledge gained from the project that can be applied to future projects.	D. Lessons Learned

2.2.11.2 Section II

One-Word Question

1. Define 'Scope' in project management.

Keyword Questions

2. What is the primary purpose of the Scope Management Plan?
3. List one tool or technique used in the Define Scope process.
4. What does WBS stand for, and why is it important in scope management?

Multiple-Choice Questions (MCQs)

5. In the context of project scope, what does the acronym WBS stand for?
   a. Work Breakdown Schedule b. Work Breakdown Structure c. Work Budget Scheduled d. Work Budget Structure
6. Which process involves subdividing project deliverables and project work into smaller, more manageable components?
   a. Collect Requirements b. Define Scope c. Create WBS d. Validate Scope
7. What is the main output of the Collect Requirements process in scope management?
   a. Scope Management Plan b. Project Scope Statement c. Requirements Traceability Matrix d. Work Breakdown Structure (WBS)

Mix and Match Question

8. Match the following processes with their descriptions:
   A. Validate Scope B. Create WBS C. Define Scope D. Control Scope
      A. Process of subdividing project deliverables and project work into smaller components.
      B. Process of formalizing acceptance of completed project deliverables.
      C. Process of developing a detailed project scope statement.
      D. Process of monitoring and controlling changes to project scope.

Fill in the Blank Questions

9. The project scope statement includes the _____, acceptance criteria, and deliverable acceptance process.
10. In the Create WBS process, the highest level of the Work Breakdown Structure is called _____.

Multiple Options Correct Questions

11. Which of the following are inputs to the Define Scope process?
    a. Project charter b. Stakeholder register c. Requirements traceability matrix d. Expert judgment
12. Which are valid components of the Project Scope Statement?
    a. Product scope description b. Project exclusions c. Constraints d. Assumptions

Mix and Match Question

13. Match the following terms related to scope management:
    A. Scope Creep B. Decomposition C. Exclusions D. Scope Verification
    1. Breaking down project deliverables into smaller, more manageable components.
    2. Formal acceptance of completed project deliverables.
    3. Gradual expansion of project scope beyond its original objectives.
    4. Clearly stating what is not included in the project scope.

Answers

One-Word Question

1. Boundaries

Keyword Questions

2. Guide Scope Activities
3. Expert Judgment
4. WBS (Breaks down deliverables)

MCQs

5. b. Work Breakdown Structure
6. c. Create WBS
7. c. Requirements Traceability Matrix

Mix and Match Question

  8. A-C, B-A, C-B, D-D

Fill in the Blank Questions

  9. Project Objectives
  10. Control Account

Multiple Options Correct Questions

  11, 12. All options correct

Mix and Match

  13. A-3, B-1, C-4, D-2

2.2.11.3 Section III

Multiple-Choice Questions

  1. What is the primary purpose of quality assurance?
    a. Detecting defects b. Preventing defects c. Correcting defects d. Ignoring defects
  2. Which of the following is a tool used in statistical quality control?
    a. Ishikawa diagram b. Pareto chart c. Control chart d. Fishbone diagram
  3. Which phase of the PDCA cycle is focused on implementing and executing the plan?
    a. Plan b. Do c. Check d. Act
  4. What is the goal of the 5 Whys technique?
    a. Identify root causes b. Generate five hypotheses c. Conduct five audits d. List five requirements
  5. In Lean Six Sigma, what does the acronym DMAIC stand for?
    a. Define, Measure, Analyze, Implement, Control b. Design, Monitor, Adjust, Implement, certify c. Detect, Mitigate, Analyze, Implement, Check d. Document, Manage, Analyze, Innovate, Communicate

One-Word/Short Answer Questions

  1. Define "Kaizen."

2. What does the term "ISO" stand for in the context of quality management standards?
3. Provide one example of a preventive quality tool.
4. What is the primary focus of the "Control" phase in DMAIC?
5. Complete the acronym "KPI," which stands for Key Performance _____.

Keyword-Type Questions

1. Name two popular quality management standards.
2. List three components of a typical Ishikawa (Fishbone) diagram.
3. Identify two categories for classifying defects during a Six Sigma project.
4. Provide keywords associated with the concept of "Total Quality Management (TQM)."
5. What are the key principles of the "Plan-Do-Check-Act" (PDCA) cycle?
6. Name one statistical tool used for measuring process capability.
7. List two primary types of variation in a process.
8. What are the four steps involved in the "Plan" phase of DMAIC?
9. Provide keywords associated with the concept of "Continuous Improvement."
10. Name three elements of a quality management system (QMS).

Answers

Multiple Choice Questions

1. b. Preventing defects
2. c. Control chart
3. b. Do
4. a. Identify root causes
5. a. Define, Measure, Analyze, Implement, Control

One-Word/Short Answer Questions

1. Continuous improvement
2. International Organization for Standardization

3. FMEA

4. Sustain

5. Indicator

Keyword Questions

1. ISO, Six Sigma
2. Cause, Effect, Category
3. Common cause, Special cause
4. Customer focus, Continuous improvement, Employee involvement
5. Plan, Do, Check, Act
6. Capability indices (Cp, Cpk)
7. Common cause, Special cause
8. Define, Measure, Analyze, Design
9. Kaizen, PDCA
10. Policies, Processes, Procedures

2.2.11.4 Section IV

Multiple-Choice Questions

1. What is the primary purpose of the Plan Resource Management process?
   a. Define project roles and responsibilities
   b. Develop the project schedule
   c. Identify project risks
   d. Create the project charter
2. Which of the following is an input to the Plan Resource Management process?
   a. Resource histogram
   b. Resource calendar
   c. Resource breakdown structure (RBS)
   d. Resource leveling
3. What is the role of expert judgment in resource planning?
   a. Prioritize risks
   b. Provide industry-specific insights
   c. Develop project schedules
   d. Control project costs

One-Word or Short Answer Questions

4. Name one output of the Plan Resource Management process.
5. What is the purpose of the Resource Management Plan?
6. Provide one example of a constraint that may impact resource planning.

Keyword-Type Questions

7. Fill in the blank: The Plan Resource Management process involves creating a _____ to guide how project resources will be utilized and managed.
8. List two tools or techniques commonly used in the Plan Resource Management process.
9. Identify one risk-related consideration during the Plan Resource Management process.

Fill in the Blank Questions

10. The project manager should collaborate with _____ managers to ensure resource availability.
11. The Resource Management Plan details how resources will be _____ and _____ throughout the project.
12. The project manager may use a Resource Breakdown Structure (RBS) to organize and classify project _____.

Answers

1. a. Define project roles and responsibilities
2. c. Resource breakdown structure (RBS)
3. b. Provide industry-specific insights
4. Staffing Management Plan
5. Guide how resources will be defined, staffed, and managed
6. Budget constraints
7. Resource Management Plan
8. Resource calendars, Expert judgment
9. Uncertainties or assumptions

10. Functional
11. Acquired, Released
12. Resources

2.2.11.5 Section V

1. Which document provides guidance on how project scope will be managed, validated, and controlled?
   a. Scope Statement
   b. WBS Dictionary
   c. Scope Management Plan
   d. Project Charter
2. What is the primary purpose of a Probability and Impact Matrix in risk management?
   a. Identify risks
   b. Assess risks
   c. Prioritize risks
   d. Develop risk responses
3. In the context of procurement management, what is the purpose of a Source Selection Criteria?
   a. Evaluate potential sellers
   b. Define project requirements
   c. Determine the critical path.
   d. Monitor project progress
4. Which tool or technique is commonly used to visually represent the project schedule?
   a. Gantt chart
   b. Fishbone diagram
   c. Pareto chart
   d. Ishikawa diagram
5. What is the primary function of a Stakeholder Register in stakeholder management?
   a. Documenting stakeholder roles
   b. Identifying potential project risks.
   c. Capturing stakeholder requirements.
   d. Recording information about project stakeholders

Answers

1. c. Scope Management Plan
2. c. Prioritize risks.
3. b. Evaluate potential sellers.
4. a. Gantt chart
5. d. Recording information about project stakeholders

2.3 Stage 3—Executing

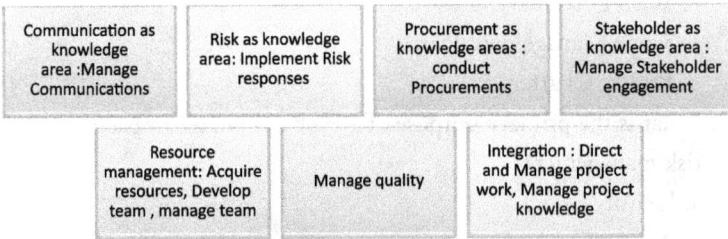

Figure 2.28 Schema for knowledge area mapping versus process (Executing)

2.3.1 Manage Communication

By effectively managing communication[9] inputs, tools, and techniques, project managers can enhance collaboration, reduce misunderstandings, and contribute to project success during the executing phase.

Project Management Plan	Project Documents	OPA : Org Process Assets	EEF	Work Performance data
• Communication Management Plan • (Provides guidance on communication handling)	• Stakeholder Register (Contains information about stakeholders, issues, and lessons learnt) • Issue Log (Identifies and documents issues) • LLR (Previous Project communication notes and experiences)	• Communication templates (standardized templates) • Communication Standards (Guidance for Communication)	• Org Culture Structure (Influence Communication channels) • Market Place Conditions (Impact Project communication)	• Project Performance Info (information about project performance)

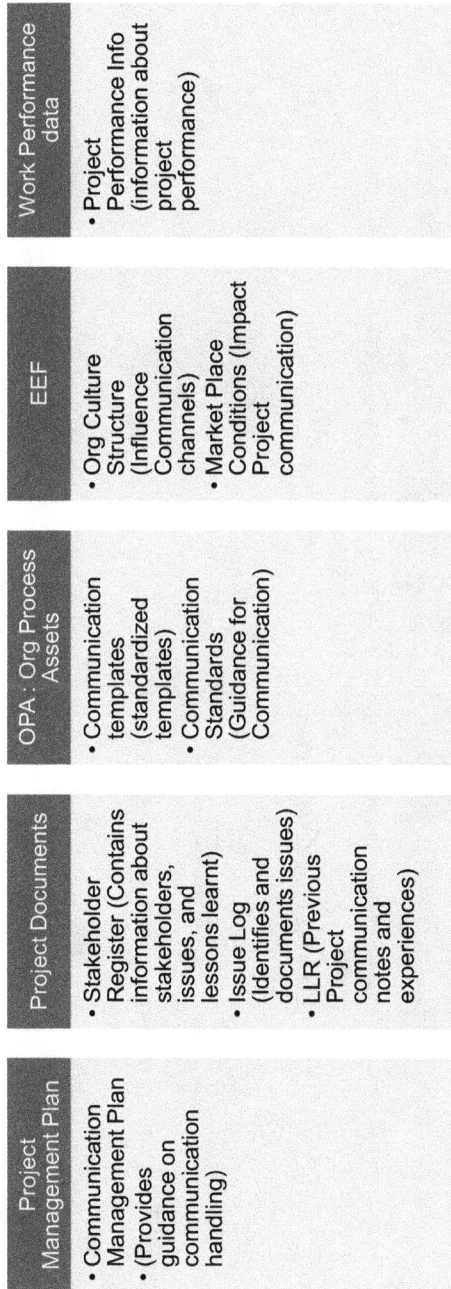

Figure 2.29 Inputs to manage communication

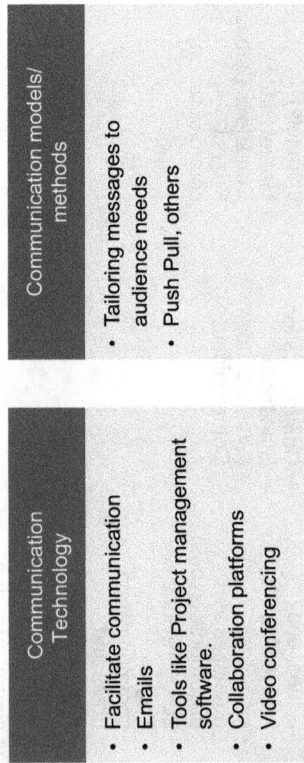

Communication Technology	Communication models/ methods
• Facilitate communication • Emails • Tools like Project management software. • Collaboration platforms • Video conferencing	• Tailoring messages to audience needs • Push Pull, others

Figure 2.30 Tools and techniques for managing communications

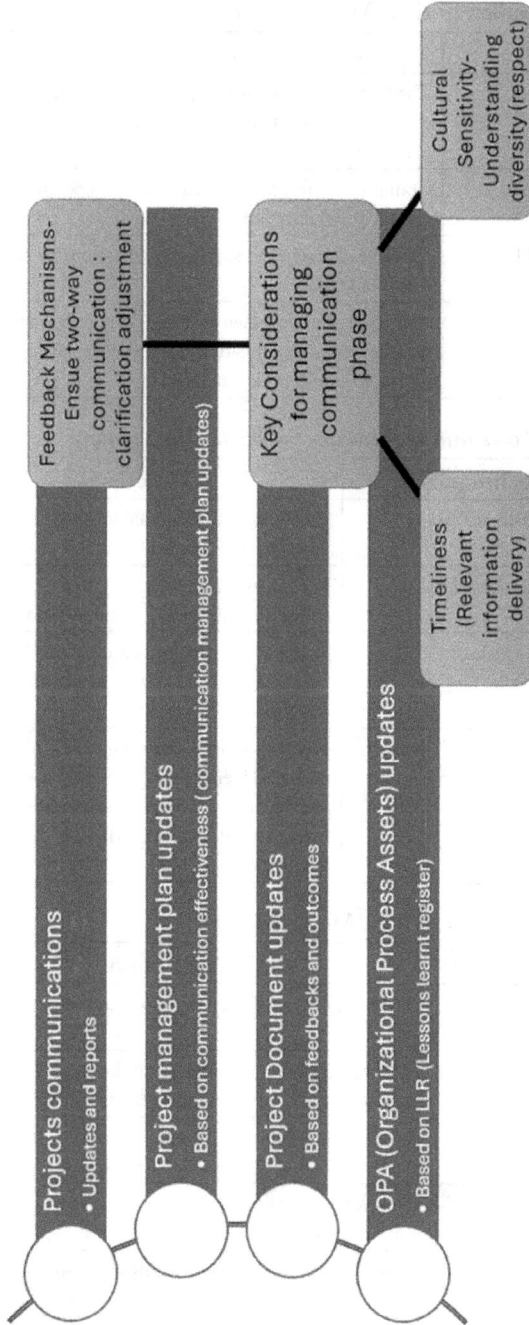

Figure 2.31 Outputs of manage communications and key considerations

Projects communications
• Updates and reports

Project management plan updates
• Based on communication effectiveness (communication management plan updates)

Project Document updates
• Based on feedbacks and outcomes

OPA (Organizational Process Assets) updates
• Based on LLR (Lessons learnt register)

Feedback Mechanisms- Ensue two-way communication : clarification adjustment

Key Considerations for managing communication phase

Cultural Sensitivity- Understanding diversity (respect)

Timeliness (Relevant information delivery)

2.3.2 Risk: Implement Risk responses

Table 2.29 Inputs to Risk Management

Inputs	Description
Project Management Plan	The Risk Management Plan, part of the project management plan, provides guidance on how risk responses should be executed.
Risk Register	Contains details on identified risks, their potential impact, and proposed responses.
Risk Response Plan	Describes the selected strategies and actions for addressing identified risks.
Project Documents, OPAs	Various project documents, such as lessons learned and stakeholder communications, can provide valuable insights for implementing risk responses.

Table 2.30 Tools and techniques for Risk Management

Tools and Techniques	Description
Strategies for Positive Risks or Opportunities	Executing actions to maximize the benefits of identified opportunities
Strategies for Negative Risks or Threats	Implementing planned actions to address and reduce the impact of identified threats
Contractual Agreements	If risks are shared with external parties, executing the agreed-upon terms and conditions in contracts
Technical Performance Measurement	Monitoring and measuring technical performance to identify variances from the plan and take corrective actions. Others include Interpersonal and team skills, PMIS, and expert Judgment

Table 2.31 Outputs to Risk Management

Outputs	Description
Work Performance Information	Provides information on the performance of risk response activities
Change Requests	May be generated if adjustments to the project management plan are needed due to the implementation of risk responses
Project Management Plan Updates	The Risk Management Plan may be updated based on the effectiveness of implemented risk responses
Project Documents Updates	The risk register and other relevant documents are updated with information on the execution of risk responses
Organizational Process Assets Updates	Lessons learned from implementing risk responses contribute to updates in organizational process assets

During the Implement Risk Responses[9] phase, the project team actively puts the planned risk response strategies into action, working to minimize the impact of threats and maximize the benefits of opportunities. Continuous monitoring and adjustment of strategies ensure the project remains aligned with its objectives in the face of uncertainties.

2.3.3 Conduct Procurements

Process Description

Conduct Procurements[9] is a project procurement management process that involves obtaining seller responses, selecting a seller, and awarding a contract. This process ensures that the project acquires goods, services, or results from external sources in accordance with the project management plan.

Figure 2.32 Key stakeholders

Table 2.32 Inputs to conducting Procurements

Inputs	Description
Project Management Plan	Contains procurement management plan, cost baseline, and scope baseline which influence the procurement process
Project Documents	Relevant documents such as the procurement statement of work, source selection criteria, and independent cost estimates
Procurement Documents	Request for Proposals (RFP), Invitation for Bids (IFB), or Request for Quotations (RFQ) are key procurement documents. All these are discussed in detail in section 2.2.9
Qualified Sellers List	A list of sellers who have been pre-qualified based on their capabilities and performance
Seller Proposals	Responses from potential sellers containing their proposed solutions, approach, and pricing
EEF, OPAs	

Table 2.33 Tools and techniques for conducting Procurements

Tools and Techniques	Description
Bidder Conferences	Meetings to clarify procurement requirements and answer questions from potential sellers
Proposal Evaluation Techniques	Criteria such as weighted scoring models or screening systems to assess and rank seller proposals
Independent Estimates, Data Analysis	Cost estimates prepared by entities not directly involved in the project, providing an objective benchmark
Expert Judgment	Input from specialists or industry experts to evaluate seller proposals and make informed decisions
Advertising	The process of announcing procurement opportunities to a wide audience, ensuring a broad pool of potential sellers

Table 2.34 Outputs to conducting Procurements

Outputs	Description
Selected Sellers	The chosen seller(s) who will provide the goods, services, or results as outlined in the contract
Procurement Agreements	Formal contracts, agreements, or purchase orders that define the terms and conditions of the procurement
Resource Calendars	Details about when and how resources will be acquired from the selected sellers
Change Requests	May arise if there are modifications or adjustments needed in the procurement process
Project Management Plan Updates	Changes to the procurement management plan, cost baseline, or schedule baseline based on the selected seller and procurement agreement

Key Considerations

Conduct Procurements is critical for ensuring that the project obtains necessary resources from external sources efficiently. It involves a thorough evaluation of seller proposals and adherence to the procurement processes outlined in the project management plan. Successful completion of this process contributes to effective project delivery and stakeholder satisfaction.

2.3.4 Manage Stakeholder Engagement

Manage Stakeholder Engagement[9] is a project stakeholder management process focused on developing strategies to engage project stakeholders effectively. This process ensures the project team collaborates with stakeholders to meet their expectations, address concerns, and foster positive relationships throughout the project life cycle.

Table 2.35 Inputs to managing stakeholder engagement

Inputs	Description
Project Management Plan	Contains the stakeholder engagement plan, communication management plan, and other relevant components
Project Documents	Stakeholder register, issue log, and other documents that provide insights into stakeholder expectations and concerns
Stakeholder Engagement Plan	Outlines the strategies and approaches for engaging stakeholders throughout the project
Work Performance Reports	Provide information on how stakeholder engagement activities are impacting project performance
Issue Log	Records concerns or issues raised by stakeholders that require attention and resolution

Table 2.36 Tools and techniques for managing stakeholder engagement

Tools and Techniques	Description
Communication Methods	Various means to engage stakeholders, including meetings, e-mails, social media, and project portals
Interpersonal and Team Skills	Effective communication, negotiation, and conflict resolution skills to foster positive relationships
Management Skills	Leadership and motivational skills to influence and guide stakeholders toward project success
Change Management Techniques	Strategies to handle and communicate changes effectively to minimize resistance
Stakeholder Engagement Assessment Matrix	Tool to assess the current and desired levels of stakeholder engagement

Table 2.37 Outputs to managing stakeholder engagement

Outputs	Description
Change Requests	May arise if stakeholder expectations or project requirements change during the engagement process
Project Management Plan Updates	Changes to the stakeholder engagement plan or other relevant sections of the project management plan
Project Documents Updates	Revision of documents like the stakeholder register to reflect the evolving stakeholder engagement status
Work Performance Information	Data on how stakeholder engagement activities influence project performance

Key Considerations

Managing Stakeholder Engagement is crucial for maintaining positive relationships with stakeholders, addressing concerns, and ensuring continued support for the project. It requires effective communication and collaboration to align project goals with stakeholder expectations. Regular assessments and updates help adapt engagement strategies based on changing project dynamics.

2.3.5 Manage Resources

Managing resources involves the following:

Figure 2.33 KPIs for managing resources

2.3.5.1 Acquire Resources

Table 2.38 Inputs to acquiring resources

Inputs	Description
Project Management Plan	Contains the Resource Management Plan, Project Staffing Plan, and Resource Calendars
Resource Calendars	Provides information on the availability and nonavailability of resources over time
Enterprise Environmental Factors (EEFs)	Factors such as market conditions and organizational culture and structure affecting resource availability
Organizational Process Assets (OPAs)	Includes historical information on resource performance and templates for resource plans

Table 2.39 Tools and techniques for acquiring resources

Knowledge Area	Project Resource Management
Tools and Techniques	Interpersonal and Team Skills: Negotiation: Communication: Influencing
	Pre-assignment: Assigning specific resources in advance based on expertise: May involve negotiations
	Virtual Teams: Utilizing resources from various locations, possibly globally: Requires communication and collaboration tools
	Interpersonal and Team Skills: Team building, Conflict resolution, Emotional intelligence
	Organizational Charts and Position Descriptions: Descriptions of roles and responsibilities: Helps in identifying suitable resources
	Networking: Building and utilizing professional networks for resource identification

Key Considerations

- Acquire Resources[9] involves obtaining and assigning project team members and other resources necessary for project completion.
- The process requires effective negotiation, communication, and collaboration skills to secure the needed resources.
- Utilizing virtual teams and networking can enhance the pool of available resources. Handling resources with emotional intelligence is required in conflicting and complex situations. *Tip: Remember servant leadership.*
- Updates to resource calendars and project documents are essential to reflect changes in resource assignments.

Output of this process area includes:

Physical resource assignments, project team assignments, resource calendars, change requests, project management plan updates, project document updates and EEFs/OPAs updates.

2.3.5.2 Develop Team

Table 2.40 Inputs to developing team

Process	Develop Team
Inputs	
Project Management Plan	Resource Management Plan
	Project Staffing Plan
Project Documents	Roles and responsibilities
	Project staff assignments
Enterprise Environmental Factors (EEFs)	Existing human resources
	Organizational culture and structure
Organizational Process Assets (OPAs)	Templates for team-building activities
	Historical information on previous projects

Table 2.41 Tools and techniques for developing team

Knowledge Area	Project Resource Management
Tools and Techniques	
Team-building Activities	Outdoor activities
	Training programs
	Team-building exercises
Interpersonal and Team Skills	Communication
	Conflict resolution
	Influencing
Recognition and Rewards	Acknowledgment of team members' efforts
	Rewards and incentives
Training	Skill development programs
	Workshops and seminars
Individual and Team Assessments	Assessing individual and collective team capabilities
Meetings	**Colocation (osmosis)** if the knowledge is tacit. This method is widely used in Agile teams or Virtual teams if the team is geographically diverse

Key Considerations[20]

- Develop Team involves enhancing the competencies and interactions of project team members to improve project performance.

- Team-building activities, training, and recognition foster a positive team environment.
- Regular assessments of individual and team performance help identify areas for improvement.
- Updates to the project management plan reflect changes in resource calendars and staffing plans due to team development activities.

Outputs

Team performance assessments, change requests, Project management Plan updates, Project document updates, EEF, and OPA updates.

2.3.5.3 Manage Team

Table 2.42 Inputs to managing team

Inputs	Description
Project Management Plan	Includes the Resource Management Plan and Staffing Management Plan detailing resource allocation and staffing strategies
Project Documents	Contains roles and responsibilities of team members and project staff assignments
Enterprise Environmental Factors (EEFs)	Considers the influence of organizational culture, structure, and existing human resources on team management
Organizational Process Assets (OPAs)	Provides templates for performance appraisals and historical data on team performance, aiding in decision making and improvement
Work Performance Reports, Team Performance Assessments	These reports and assessments assist in evaluating team members' performance and providing feedback for improvement

Table 2.43 Tools and outputs to managing team

Knowledge Area	Project Resource Management
Tools and Techniques	• Interpersonal and team skills: Facilitate effective communication, conflict resolution, and team collaboration • PMIS (Project Management Information System): Utilize software tools for resource tracking, allocation, and reporting
Outputs	• Change requests: Requests for modifications to the project resources or management approach • Project Management Plan updates: Revisions to resource management plans based on project needs or changes • EEF (Enterprise Environmental Factors), OPA (Organizational Process Assets) updates: Updates to reflect changes in organizational culture, available resources, or processes • Project document updates: Revisions to project documents such as staffing plans, roles and responsibilities, and resource assignments

Key Considerations[20]

- Manage Team involves tracking team performance, resolving conflicts, and ensuring the team stays motivated and productive.
- Regular observations and conversations help understand team dynamics and promptly address any emerging issues.
- Performance appraisals and feedback contribute to continuous improvement and alignment with project objectives.
- Changes to the project management plan may be required to adjust resource allocations or roles based on team performance assessments.

2.3.6 Manage Quality

Table 2.44 Inputs, tools, and outputs to managing quality

Knowledge Area	Project Quality Management
Inputs	
1. Project Management Plan	• Quality Management Plan: Defines quality policies, procedures, and responsibilities • Process Improvement Plan: Describes steps for process improvement
2. Quality Metrics	• Defined quality metrics for the project • Benchmarking results for comparison

Table 2.44 (Continued)

Knowledge Area	Project Quality Management
3. Quality Control Measurements	• Results from quality control measurements • Data on defects, errors, or issues
4. Project Documents	• Lessons Learned: Insights from previous projects to improve quality • Risk Register: Identifies potential quality risks
5. Agreements	• Any agreements with suppliers or external partners related to quality
Tools and Techniques	
1. Quality Audits	• Systematic examination of the project to determine compliance with defined quality standards
2. Process Analysis	• Evaluating processes to identify areas for improvement; • Analyzing data to assess process performance
3. Quality Management and Control Tools	• Tools such as flowcharts, checklists, and control charts for managing and controlling quality
4. Seven Basic Quality Tools	• Tools like Pareto diagrams, cause-and-effect diagrams, and histograms for quality improvement
5. Statistical Sampling	• Selecting a sample from the project for inspection and testing • Statistical techniques for analyzing sample data
6. Design for X	• Focusing on specific aspects like reliability, safety, or manufacturability during the design phase • Enhancing quality by considering various factors
7. Problem Solving	• Methods like root cause analysis to identify and address underlying causes of quality issues
Outputs	
1. Quality Reports	• Summarizes results of quality control measurements; • Highlights any nonconformities or issues
2. Change Requests	• Proposes changes to address quality issues • May include adjustments to processes, procedures, or plans
3. Project Management Plan Updates	• Quality Management Plan updates • Process Improvement Plan updates
4. Project Documents Updates	• Lessons Learned: Documenting insights for future projects • Risk Register: Updating with lessons learned and new risks

Key Considerations[20]

- Manage Quality ensures that the project meets the defined quality standards and takes corrective actions if quality issues arise.

- Quality audits and various tools help identify and address quality concerns throughout the project life cycle.
- Outputs like quality reports and change requests contribute to continuous improvement and adherence to quality objectives.

2.3.7 Manage Integration

Table 2.45 Inputs, tools, and outputs to managing integration: direct and manage project work

Knowledge Area	Project Integration Management
Inputs	
1. Project Management Plan	• Integrated Baseline: Snapshot of the project's approved scope, schedule, and cost • Scope Baseline: Detailed project scope statement and associated WBS • Schedule Baseline: Approved project schedule • Cost Baseline: Approved project budgets
2. Project Documents	• Project Schedule: Planned dates for project activities • Project Funding Requirements: Details about financial needs • Resource Calendars: Information about resource availability • Risk Register: Identifies potential project risks • Issue Log: Documents ongoing issues • Approved Change Requests
3. Enterprise Environmental Factors (EEFs)	• External factors influencing project work direction and management • Marketplace conditions, industry standards, and so on
4. Organizational Process Assets (OPAs)	• Organizational standard processes, policies, and procedures • Templates, historical information, lessons learned
Tools and Techniques	
1. Expert Judgment	• Input from knowledgeable individuals or groups • Industry experts, team members, or stakeholders provide insights
2. Project Management Information System (PMIS)	• Software tools/systems used for project management • Assist in planning, executing, and closing projects
3. Meetings	• Formal or informal discussions to coordinate project work • Facilitate communication among team members and stakeholders

Table 2.45 (Continued)

Knowledge Area	Project Integration Management
4. Communication Methods	• Various methods to convey information within the project team • Meetings, e-mails, reports, and so on
Outputs	
1. Deliverables	• Tangible results/items produced as part of project work • Interim or final deliverables
2. Work Performance Data	• Raw observations and measurements collected during project execution • Foundation for performance reporting and analysis
3. Issue Log Updates	• Documentation of any new issues identified during project work
4. Change Requests	• Proposals for modifications to project documents, deliverables, or baselines • Scope changes, schedule adjustments, or resource reallocations
5. Project Management Plan Updates	• Any modifications to the project management plan resulting from project work • Updates to scope, schedule, or cost baselines if necessary

Key Considerations[20]

• Direct and Manage Project Work involves executing the project management plan to produce project deliverables.
• It ensures that project work is performed efficiently and effectively, following the defined processes and standards.
• Outputs such as deliverables and work performance data contribute to ongoing monitoring and control of the project.

Table 2.46 Inputs, tools, and outputs to managing integration—Managing project knowledge

Knowledge Area	Project Integration Management
Inputs	
1. Project Management Plan	• Contains information on how knowledge will be captured, shared, and used throughout the project • Describes roles and responsibilities related to knowledge management

(Continued)

Table 2.46 (Continued)

Knowledge Area	Project Integration Management
2. Project Documents	• Lessons Learned Register: Repository of documented knowledge from previous projects • Risk Register: Information on identified risks, including knowledge-related risks • Stakeholder Register: Information on stakeholders, including communication preferences
3. Enterprise Environmental Factors (EEFs)	• Factors external to the project impacting knowledge management • Organizational culture, existing knowledge repositories, collaboration tools
4. Organizational Process Assets (OPAs)	• Historical information and lessons learned from previous projects • Existing knowledge management policies, procedures, guidelines
Tools and Techniques	
1. Data Analysis	• Examining data to identify patterns, trends, or insights related to project knowledge • Analyzing lessons learned, feedback, or other knowledge-related data
2. Knowledge Management Techniques	• Strategies and methods for capturing, organizing, and disseminating knowledge • Documentation, databases, collaboration platforms, social media
3. Interpersonal and Team Skills	• Communication, collaboration, relationship-building skills • Facilitate sharing and transfer of knowledge among team members
4. Knowledge Management (KM) Tools	• Software and technologies facilitating knowledge management • Document repositories, wikis, knowledge bases, collaborative platforms
Outputs	
1. Lessons Learned	• Insights gained from the project applicable to future projects • Captures positive and negative experiences for future decision making
2. Project Management Plan Updates	• Updates to the project management plan based on knowledge gained during project execution • Improvements to knowledge management processes
3. Project Documents Updates	• Updates to relevant project documents based on lessons learned and other knowledge • May include updates to the risk register, stakeholder register, and so on

Key Considerations

- Managing Project Knowledge focuses on creating, sharing, and applying project knowledge to improve future performance.
- It involves continuously identifying, documenting, and disseminating lessons learned and best practices.
- Effective knowledge management enhances decision making, reduces risks, and improves organizational learning.

2.3.8 Question and Answer Based on "Stage—Execution"

1. **Project Team Collaboration**
   - You notice a lack of collaboration among team members. What action should you take to address this during the executing phase?
   a. Document the issue for future reference. b. Hold a team-building workshop. c. Ignore it, as it might resolve on its own. d. Escalate the issue to senior management.

2. **Quality Assurance**
   - During execution, you discover that the quality of deliverables is not meeting the standards set in the project plan. What should you do?
   a. Proceed as planned; the quality can be addressed later. b. Inform the team, conduct a root cause analysis, and take corrective action. c. Update the project plan to lower quality expectations. d. Seek approval from stakeholders for the lower quality standards.

3. **Resource Allocation**
   - You realize that a critical resource is consistently overloaded with tasks. What is the best course of action during execution?
   a. Leave it to the resource to manage workload. b. Reallocate tasks among team members. c. Extend project timelines to accommodate the workload. d. Hire additional resources to ease the workload.

4. **Communication Breakdown**
   - Stakeholders are complaining about a lack of project updates. How can you address this issue during execution?
   a. Ignore the complaints; stakeholders will be informed in due time. b. Schedule more frequent status meetings. c. Revise the communication plan and ensure timely updates. d. Escalate the issue to project sponsors.

5. **Scope Creep**
   - A stakeholder requests additional features that were not part of the initial scope. How should you handle this situation?
   a. Incorporate the new features without adjusting the project scope. b. Communicate the impact on scope, time, and cost before proceeding. c. Ignore the request to avoid project delays. d. Delegate the decision to the project team.

6. **Risk Response**
   - A risk you identified during planning has occurred. What is the next step in the executing phase?
   a. Implement the planned risk response. b. Document the risk for lessons learned. c. Revisit the risk management plan. d. Ignore the risk and proceed with execution.

7. **Supplier Performance**
   - One of your key suppliers is consistently delivering subpar materials. How can you manage this issue during the executing phase?
   a. Terminate the supplier contract immediately. b. Continue with the current supplier to avoid delays. c. Work closely with the supplier to address performance issues. d. Ignore the issue and adjust project expectations.

8. **Conflict Resolution**
   - Two team members are frequently in conflict, impacting project progress. How should you address this during execution?
   a. Let them resolve the conflict on their own. b. Ignore the conflict until it becomes a major issue. c. Mediate the conflict and work toward a resolution. d. Replace one of the team members to eliminate the conflict.

9. **Client Expectations**
   - The client has misunderstood project deliverables, leading to dissatisfaction. What should you do to manage client expectations during execution?
   a. Blame the client for the misunderstanding. b. Revise the project plan to align with client expectations. c. Communicate clearly and seek agreement on project scope. d. Ignore the client's concerns, as they will likely change.

10. **Resource Constraints**
   - Your project is facing budget constraints, and resources are limited. What action should you take during execution?
   a. Seek additional funding from stakeholders. b. Cut down on project scope to match available resources. c. Ignore the budget constraints and proceed as planned. d. Postpone the project until additional funds are available.

11. **Client Participation**
   - The client is not actively participating in project activities, hindering decision-making. How should you address this during the executing phase?
   a. Continue with the project and make decisions independently. b. Encourage client participation through regular updates and meetings. c. Exclude the client from project activities to avoid delays. d. Escalate the issue to higher management for resolution.

12. **Change Control**
   - A change request that could significantly impact the project has been submitted during execution. What should you do first?
   a. Implement the change without formal approval.
   b. Review the change request and assess its impact. c. Ignore the change request to maintain project stability. d. Reject the change request without further consideration.

13. **Task Dependencies**
   - You discover that tasks are not progressing smoothly due to unclear dependencies. How can you address this issue during execution?
   a. Ignore the dependencies and proceed with tasks. b. Identify and clarify task dependencies with the team. c. Redefine the

project schedule to remove dependencies. d. Escalate the issue to senior management for resolution.

14. **Quality Control**
    - Quality control measures indicate that deliverables are consistently below quality standards. What is the appropriate action during execution?
    a. Ignore the quality control results to avoid delays. b. Revise quality standards to match current deliverables. c. Implement corrective actions to improve deliverable quality. d. Document the quality issues for future reference.

15. **Team Morale**
    - Team morale is low due to extended working hours. How can you address this issue during execution?
    a. Encourage the team to continue working long hours to meet deadlines. b. Provide additional compensation to motivate the team. c. Reallocate tasks to balance workload and reduce stress. d. Ignore the morale issue and focus on project timelines.

16. **Client Feedback**
    - The client provides feedback suggesting changes to the project plan. How should you incorporate this feedback during execution?
    a. Ignore the feedback as it might cause delays. b. Immediately implement all client suggestions. c. Evaluate the feedback, discuss with the team, and implement agreed-upon changes. d. Reject the feedback without further consideration.

17. **Resource Constraints**
    - Key resources are not available as planned, impacting project progress. What should you do during execution?
    a. Continue with available resources to avoid delays.
    b. Delay project activities until the resources are available.
    c. Reallocate tasks to other team members. d. Escalate the resource issue to senior management.

18. **Communication Delays**
    - You realize that communication is delayed, affecting decision-making. How can you address this during execution?

a. Continue with the current communication plan. b. Increase the frequency of communication updates. c. Revise the communication plan to expedite information flow. d. Ignore the communication delays to avoid disruptions.

19. **Technology Issues**

- Unexpected technology issues are hindering project progress. What is the best approach during execution?
  a. Continue with the current technology and manage issues as they arise. b. Seek immediate technological solutions to resolve issues. c. Ignore technology issues as they are common in projects. d. Inform stakeholders about the technology challenges and adjust project expectations.

20. **Regulatory Compliance**

- You discover that the project is not fully compliant with relevant regulations. How should you handle this during execution?
  a. Continue with the project, ignoring regulatory compliance. b. Seek legal advice to understand the implications. c. Revise the project plan to align with regulations. d. Document the noncompliance and inform stakeholders.

Answers and Their Explanation

1. **Answer: b**
   - Holding a team-building workshop is a proactive approach to address collaboration issues and improve team dynamics.

2. **Answer: b**
   - Informing the team, conducting a root cause analysis, and taking corrective action align with quality management principles.

3. **Answer: b**
   - Reallocating tasks among team members is a strategic move to balance workload and ensure efficient resource utilization.

4. **Answer: c**
   - Revising the communication plan to ensure timely updates addresses the stakeholder's concerns about project communication.

5. **Answer: b**
   - Communicating the impact on scope, time, and cost before proceeding ensures transparency and manages stakeholder expectations.

6. **Answer: a**
   - Implementing the planned risk response is the appropriate action when an identified risk materializes.

7. **Answer: c**
   - Working closely with the supplier to address performance issues is a collaborative approach to managing supplier relationships.

8. **Answer: c**
   - Mediating the conflict and working toward a resolution promotes a healthy team environment.

9. **Answer: c**
   - Communicating clearly and seeking agreement on project scope helps manage client expectations and avoid misunderstandings.

10. **Answer: b**
    - Cutting down on project scope to match available resources is a strategic response to budget constraints.

11. **Answer: b**
    - Encouraging client participation through regular updates and meetings facilitates better decision making.

12. **Answer: b**
    - Reviewing the change request and assessing its impact is the first step in the change control process.

13. **Answer: b**
    - Identifying and clarifying task dependencies with the team ensures smooth progress of project tasks.

14. **Answer: c**
    - Implementing corrective actions to improve deliverable quality is essential for meeting project standards.

15. **Answer: c**
   - Reallocating tasks to balance workload and reduce stress addresses the low morale issue in the team.

16. **Answer: c**
   - Evaluating the client feedback, discussing with the team, and implementing agreed-upon changes is a balanced approach.

17. **Answer: d**
   - Escalating the resource issue to senior management is necessary for resolving key resource constraints.

18. **Answer: c**
   - Revising the communication plan to expedite information flow addresses delays and ensures timely communication.

19. **Answer: b**
   - Seeking immediate technological solutions to resolve issues is a proactive response to unexpected technology challenges.

20. **Answer: b**
   - Seeking legal advice to understand the implications of noncompliance is a crucial step in addressing regulatory issues.

2.4 Stage 4—Monitor and Control

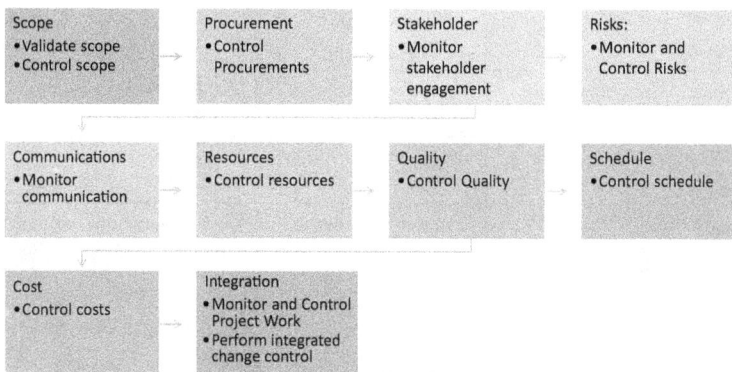

Scope	Procurement	Stakeholder	Risks:
• Validate scope	• Control Procurements	• Monitor stakeholder engagement	• Monitor and Control Risks
• Control scope			

Communications	Resources	Quality	Schedule
• Monitor communication	• Control resources	• Control Quality	• Control schedule

Cost	Integration
• Control costs	• Monitor and Control Project Work
	• Perform integrated change control

Figure 2.34 Phases for Stage—Monitor and control

Table 2.47 ITTO—Process: Validate scope

Inputs	Tools and Techniques	Outputs
Project Management Plan	Inspection	Accepted Deliverables
Requirements Documentation	Group Decision Making	Change Requests
Requirements Traceability Matrix		Project Document Updates
Verified Deliverables		Work Performance Information
Work Performance Data		

Table 2.48 ITTO—Process: Control scope

Inputs	Tools and Techniques	Outputs
Project Management Plan	Variance Analysis	Work Performance Information
Requirements Documentation	Trend Analysis	Change Requests
Requirements Traceability Matrix	Group Decision Making	Project Management Plan Updates
Work Performance Data	Data Analysis	Project Document Updates
Organizational Process Assets (OPA)		

Table 2.49 ITTO—Process: Control Procurements

Inputs	Tools and Techniques	Outputs
Project Management Plan	Procurement Performance Reviews	Procurement Documentation
Procurement Documents	Inspections and Audits	Approved Change Requests
Agreements	Claims Administration	Work Performance Information
Approved Change Requests		Close Procurements
Work Performance Data		OPA, Project Document Updates

Table 2.50 ITTO—Process: Monitor stakeholder engagement

Inputs	Tools and Techniques	Outputs
Project Management Plan	Information Distribution	Work Performance Information
Stakeholder Engagement Plan	Stakeholder Meetings	Change Requests
Work Performance Data	Analytical Techniques	Project Management Plan Updates
Change Requests		
Project Documents		

Table 2.51 ITTO—Process: Monitor and control risks

Inputs	Tools and Techniques	Outputs
Project Management Plan	Risk Audits	Work Performance Information
Risk Register	Variance and Trend Analysis	Change Requests
Work Performance Data	Technical Performance Measurement	Project Management Plan Updates
Work Performance Information	Reserve Analysis	
Change Requests		

Table 2.52 ITTO—Process: Monitor communication

Inputs	Tools and Techniques	Outputs
Project Management Plan	Communication Methods	Work Performance Information
Communications Management Plan	Information Distribution	Change Requests
Work Performance Data	Performance Reporting	Project Management Plan Updates
Issue Log	PMIS, Expert Judgment	Project Document
Change Requests	Data Representation	

Table 2.53 ITTO—Process: Control resources

Inputs	Tools and Techniques	Outputs
Project Management Plan	Resource Leveling	Work Performance Information
Resource Calendars	Team Building	Change Requests
Work Performance Data	Interpersonal and Team Skills	Project Management Plan Updates
Issue Log	Problem Solving, PMIS	Project Documents, Agreements

Table 2.54 ITTO—Process: Control quality

Inputs	Tools and Techniques	Outputs
Project Management Plan	Statistical Sampling	Quality Control Measurements
Quality Metrics	Inspection	Validated Changes
Quality Control Measurements	Control Charts	Work Performance Information
Work Performance Data	Data Gathering, Representation, Analysis	Project Document Updates
Approved Change Requests	Testing/Product Evaluations	

Table 2.55 ITTO—Process: Control schedule

Inputs	Tools and Techniques	Outputs
Project Management Plan	Schedule Compression	Work Performance Information
Schedule Baseline	Resource Leveling, Optimization	Change Requests
Work Performance Data	What-If Analysis	Project Management Plan Updates
Approved Change Requests	Critical Path Method, Leads and Lags	Schedule Forecasts

Table 2.56 ITTO—Process: Control costs

Inputs	Tools and Techniques	Outputs
Project Management Plan	Earned Value Management	Work Performance Information
Cost Baseline, Project Funding Requirements	Forecasting	Change Requests
Work Performance Data	To-Complete Performance Index	Project Management Plan Updates
Approved Change Requests		Cost Forecasts

Table 2.57 ITTO—Integration: Monitor and control project work

Inputs	Tools and Techniques	Outputs
Project Management Plan	Performance Reviews	Work Performance Information
Work Performance Data	Issue Log	Change Requests
Issue Log	Change Control Tools	Project Management Plan Updates
Change Requests		Project Documents Updates

Table 2.58 ITTO—Integration: Perform integrated change control

Inputs	Tools and Techniques	Outputs
Project Management Plan	Change Control Board	Approved Change Requests
Work Performance Data	Expert Judgment	Project Management Plan Updates
Change Requests	Meetings	Project Documents Updates
Project Documents		Enterprise Environmental Factors

Note: **These are simplified representations, and the actual inputs and outputs can vary based on project specifics.**[9,21,20]

2.4.1 Question and Answer Based on "Stage-Monitor and Control"

1. **Scenario:** During the monitoring and control phase, the project manager notices that the project is behind schedule. What should be the immediate action?
   a. Update the project schedule for internal reference only.
   b. Analyze the causes of the delay and implement corrective actions.
   c. Ignore the delay and focus on other aspects of the project.
   d. Seek additional budget to accommodate the delays.
   Answer: b. Analyze the causes of the delay and implement corrective actions.

2. **Scenario:** A stakeholder expresses dissatisfaction with a project deliverable during the monitoring phase. What is the appropriate response?
   a. Ignore the feedback, assuming it is subjective.
   b. Document the feedback and discuss it in the next project team meeting.
   c. Delay addressing the concern until the next project phase.
   d. Inform the stakeholder that changes are not possible at this stage.
   Answer: b. Document the feedback and discuss it in the next project team meeting.

3. **Scenario:** Quality control reports indicate a decline in product quality. What should the project manager do first?
   a. Revise the quality standards for the project.
   b. Communicate the issue to the project team and initiate corrective actions.
   c. Seek additional budget to invest in higher-quality materials.
   d. Downplay the quality concern to avoid causing panic.
   Answer: b. Communicate the issue to the project team and initiate corrective actions.

4. **Scenario:** During the control phase, it is identified that the project expenses are consistently exceeding the planned budget. What is the appropriate course of action?
   a. Adjust the budget to accommodate the overruns.

b. Investigate the root causes of the budget overruns and take corrective actions.

c. Reduce the scope of the project to align with the budget.

d. Ignore the budget overruns, as they are common in projects.

Answer: b. Investigate the root causes of the budget overruns and take corrective actions.

5. **Scenario:** The project team identifies potential risks that were not initially considered during the planning phase. What should the project manager do?

a. Ignore the new risks as they were not identified during planning.

b. Include the new risks in the risk register and develop appropriate responses.

c. Downplay the significance of the new risks to avoid causing concern.

d. Defer the consideration of new risks until the next project phase.

Answer: b. Include the new risks in the risk register and develop appropriate responses.

6. **Scenario:** A key team member resigns unexpectedly during the monitoring phase. What is the immediate action?

a. Delay project activities until a replacement is found.

b. Assess the impact on the project schedule and allocate tasks to remaining team members.

c. Ignore the departure, assuming it won't affect the project significantly.

d. Seek legal action against the departing team member.

Answer: b. Assess the impact on the project schedule and allocate tasks to remaining team members.

7. **Scenario:** Stakeholders request additional features that were not part of the original project scope. How should the project manager handle this situation?

a. Include the new features without assessing their impact.

b. Assess the impact on the project scope, schedule, and budget before deciding.

c. Politely reject the stakeholder requests to avoid scope creep.

d. Include the new features without informing the project team.

Answer: b. Assess the impact on the project scope, schedule, and budget before deciding.

8. **Scenario:** The project manager receives conflicting reports on the progress of a critical task. What is the appropriate action?

a. Base decisions on the more optimistic report to maintain positivity.

b. Investigate the discrepancies and clarify the actual status of the task.

c. Ignore the conflicting reports, assuming they will balance out in the end.

d. Immediately escalate the issue to senior management for resolution.

Answer: b. Investigate the discrepancies and clarify the actual status of the task.

9. **Scenario:** During the control phase, a stakeholder requests changes to the project schedule. What is the project manager's response?

a. Immediately implement the changes without further analysis.

b. Assess the impact on the project schedule and discuss it with relevant stakeholders.

c. Reject the stakeholder request to maintain the project timeline.

d. Consult only the project team before making any decisions.

Answer: b. Assess the impact on the project schedule and discuss it with relevant stakeholders.

10. **Scenario:** The quality control team identifies a defect in a critical deliverable. What should the project manager do first?

a. Downplay the severity of the defect to avoid project delays.

b. Initiate a thorough investigation into the root causes of the defect.

c. Inform the client about the defect immediately.

d. Ignore the defect, assuming it won't affect the overall project quality.

Answer: b. Initiate a thorough investigation into the root causes of the defect.

11. **Scenario:** A stakeholder raises concerns about the accuracy of project status reports during the control phase. How should the project manager address this?

    a. Ignore the stakeholder concerns as they may be misinformed.

    b. Review the project status reporting process and make necessary improvements.

    c. Conceal certain project issues to maintain a positive image.

    d. Immediately escalate the concerns to senior management for resolution.

    Answer: b. Review the project status reporting process and make necessary improvements.

12. **Scenario:** Key performance indicators (KPIs) indicate that the project consistently exceeds planned costs. What should the project manager do?

    a. Revise the cost estimates to align with the actual expenses.

    b. Analyze the cost overruns and implement corrective actions.

    c. Downplay the cost concerns to avoid panic among stakeholders.

    d. Seek additional budget without a detailed analysis.

    Answer: b. Analyze the cost overruns and implement corrective actions.

13. **Scenario:** A team member reports a potential conflict of interest related to a procurement decision. What should the project manager do?

    a. Ignore the conflict of interest to maintain team harmony.

    b. Investigate the reported conflict of interest and take appropriate actions.

    c. Delay the procurement decision until the conflict is resolved.

    d. Inform only senior management about the reported conflict.

    Answer: b. Investigate the reported conflict of interest and take appropriate actions.

14. **Scenario:** During a stakeholder meeting, the client expresses dissatisfaction with the project's progress. How should the project manager respond?

    a. Downplay the client's concerns to maintain a positive image.

    b. Acknowledge the concerns and present a plan to address them.

c. Ignore the client's feedback, assuming it is based on misinformation.

d. Immediately terminate the project to avoid further dissatisfaction.

Answer: b. Acknowledge the concerns and present a plan to address them.

15. **Scenario:** A risk that was identified and documented during the planning phase materializes. What is the next step for the project manager?

a. Ignore the risk as it was already identified during planning.

b. Implement the response plan developed during the planning phase.

c. Downplay the significance of the risk to avoid causing concern.

d. Defer the response to the risk until the next project phase.

Answer: b. Implement the response plan developed during the planning phase.

16. **Scenario:** The project manager receives feedback from the quality control team about the need for additional training. What is the appropriate response?

a. Disregard the feedback, assuming the team is already trained adequately.

b. Provide the necessary training to address identified skill gaps.

c. Delay the training until the next project phase.

d. Replace team members to avoid investing in training.

Answer: b. Provide the necessary training to address identified skill gaps.

17. **Scenario:** The project manager notices that a team member consistently fails to meet deadlines during the monitoring phase. What is the appropriate action?

a. Ignore the issue, assuming it won't affect the overall project timeline.

b. Conduct a performance review with the team member and discuss the issue.

c. Replace the team member without further investigation.

d. Conceal the performance issue to avoid team demotivation.

Answer: b. Conduct a performance review with the team member and discuss the issue.

18. **Scenario:** The project manager receives a change request that was not part of the original scope. What is the first step?

    a. Implement the change immediately to satisfy the requester.

    b. Evaluate the change request and assess its impact on scope, schedule, and budget.

    c. Reject the change request to avoid scope creep.

    d. Seek approval from senior management before considering the change.

    Answer: b. Evaluate the change request and assess its impact on scope, schedule, and budget.

19. **Scenario:** The project manager identifies a deviation from the project's quality standards during the control phase. What is the immediate action?

    a. Downplay the deviation to avoid negative attention.

    b. Investigate the root causes of the deviation and implement corrective actions.

    c. Ignore the quality deviation as it may not impact the overall project.

    d. Seek legal advice before taking any corrective actions.

    Answer: b. Investigate the root causes of the deviation and implement corrective actions.

20. **Scenario:** Stakeholders request additional project documentation during the control phase. What is the project manager's response?

    a. Provide the requested documentation without further analysis.

    b. Assess the need for additional documentation and discuss it with stakeholders.

    c. Reject the request, stating that existing documentation is sufficient.

    d. Delay providing the documentation to maintain control over project information.

    Answer: b. Assess the need for additional documentation and discuss it with stakeholders.

2.5 Stage 5—Closing

Closing[9] a project involves completing all activities and deliverables, obtaining customer or stakeholder acceptance, and formally closing out the project.

> **Inputs:** Project charter, Project management plan, Project documents, Accepted deliverables, business documents, agreements, procurement documentation, OPAs
> **Tools and Techniques:** Expert Judgment, Data analysis, meetings
> **Outputs:** Project documents updates, Final product, service or result transition, Final report, OPA updates

Here are the key steps to close a project:

1. **Review and Verify Project Objectives**
   - Ensure that all project objectives and requirements have been met.
   - Verify that all deliverables are complete and meet the specified criteria.

2. **Customer or Stakeholder Acceptance**
   - Obtain formal acceptance from the customer or key stakeholders.
   - Address any outstanding issues or concerns raised by the customer.

3. **Finalize Project Documentation**
   - Complete and update all project documentation.
   - Archive project files and records for future reference.

4. **Conduct Lessons Learned**
   - Hold a lesson-learned session with the project team.
   - Document successes, challenges, and recommendations for future projects.

5. **Release Project Resources**
   - Release team members from project responsibilities.
   - Ensure that all resources, including equipment and facilities, are returned or released.

- Conducting LLR should be done before releasing resources, as they are important while preparing LLR.

6. **Complete Financial Closure**
   - Finalize all financial aspects of the project, including closing contracts and processing final payments.
   - Ensure that all project expenses and budgetary aspects are reconciled.

7. **Communication and Reporting**
   - Inform all stakeholders, including team members, customers, and management, about the project's successful completion.
   - Provide a final project report highlighting achievements, challenges, and outcomes.

8. **Close Procurements**
   - Ensure that all contracts and procurements associated with the project are officially closed.
   - Complete any remaining contractual obligations.

9. **Celebrate Success**
   - Acknowledge and celebrate the successful completion of the project with the project team.
   - Recognize individual and team contributions.

10. **Project Closure Documentation**
    - Document the project closure, including the formal acceptance, financial closure, and lessons learned.
    - Ensure that all required approvals and signatures are obtained.

11. **Handover to Operations or Maintenance (if applicable)**
    - If the project involves a product or service transition, ensure a smooth handover to the operations or maintenance team.

12. **Archive and Store Project Information**
    - Archive project documentation and store it in a secure and accessible location for future reference.
    - Maintain records for audits or potential future needs.

13. **Formal Project Closure Meeting**
    - Conduct a formal project closure meeting to officially close the project and thank all involved parties.

14. **Post-Implementation Review (if applicable)**
    - For projects with a product or service implementation, conduct a post-implementation review to assess performance and address any issues.

15. **Follow Organizational Closure Procedures**
    - Follow any specific closure procedures outlined by the organization or industry standards.

By following these steps, you ensure that the project is formally closed and all necessary documentation is completed. Project closure is essential for reflecting on the project's success, identifying areas for improvement, and transitioning the project's outcomes appropriately.

2.5.1 Question and Answer based on "Stage-Closing"

1. **Scenario:** The project manager realizes that some project activities were not documented in the final project report during the closing phase. What should be the immediate action?
    a. Ignore the oversight, assuming it won't affect the overall project closure.
    b. Amend the final project report to include the missing activities.
    c. Delay the project closure until all activities are documented.
    d. Seek approval from senior management before taking any action.

    Answer: b. Amend the final project report to include the missing activities.

2. **Scenario:** The client expresses satisfaction with the project deliverables during the closing phase. What is the project manager's response?
    a. Ignore the client's feedback, assuming it is not necessary for closure.
    b. Document the client's satisfaction as part of the project closure report.
    c. Politely reject the client's feedback to avoid prolonged discussions.

    d. Seek additional feedback from other stakeholders before considering closure.

Answer: b. Document the client's satisfaction as part of the project closure report.

3. **Scenario:** A team member raises concerns about the accuracy of project documentation during the closing phase. What is the appropriate response?

    a. Disregard the team member's concerns, assuming they are misinformed.

    b. Review the project documentation and make necessary corrections.

    c. Delay the project closure until all documentation concerns are resolved.

    d. Inform only senior management about the reported concerns.

Answer: b. Review the project documentation and make necessary corrections.

4. **Scenario:** The project manager discovers that some project expenses were not properly accounted for in the financial closure. What is the immediate action?

    a. Conceal the oversight to avoid financial scrutiny.

    b. Amend the financial closure documents to include the missing expenses.

    c. Seek legal advice before addressing the financial oversight.

    d. Delay the financial closure until all expenses are properly accounted for.

Answer: b. Amend the financial closure documents to include the missing expenses.

5. **Scenario:** During the closing phase, the project manager receives requests for additional features from stakeholders. What is the appropriate response?

    a. Implement the additional features to satisfy the stakeholders.

    b. Assess the impact on the project closure and discuss it with stakeholders.

    c. Reject the stakeholder requests to avoid scope creep.

    d. Implement the additional features without further analysis.

Answer: c. Reject the stakeholder requests to avoid scope creep.

6. **Scenario:** The project manager identifies outstanding contracts that were not closed during the closing phase. What is the next step?

    a. Ignore the outstanding contracts, assuming they are not critical for closure.

    b. Initiate the closure of the remaining contracts to complete the project closure.

    c. Delay the project closure until all outstanding contracts are resolved.

    d. Inform only senior management about the outstanding contracts.

    Answer: b. Initiate the closure of the remaining contracts to complete the project closure.

7. **Scenario:** Stakeholders express concerns about the communication process during the project. What is the project manager's response during the closing phase?

    a. Ignore the stakeholder concerns, assuming they are not relevant for closure.

    b. Document the stakeholder concerns as lessons learned for future projects.

    c. Delay the project closure until all communication concerns are addressed.

    d. Conceal the communication concerns to avoid a negative image.

    Answer: b. Document the stakeholder concerns as lessons learned for future projects.

8. **Scenario:** The project manager receives feedback from the team about the need for additional training during the closing phase. What is the appropriate response?

    a. Disregard the team's feedback, assuming they are already trained adequately.

    b. Provide the necessary training to address identified skill gaps.

    c. Delay the training until the next project phase.

    d. Replace team members to avoid investing in training.

    Answer: b. Provide the necessary training to address identified skill gaps.

9. **Scenario:** The project manager realizes that key project documents were not archived properly during the closing phase. What is the immediate action?

   a. Conceal the oversight to avoid scrutiny.

   b. Archive the documents properly to ensure compliance with closure processes.

   c. Delay the project closure until all documents are properly archived.

   d. Seek legal advice before addressing the document archiving issue.

   Answer: b. Archive the documents properly to ensure compliance with closure processes.

10. **Scenario:** A stakeholder requests changes to the final project report during the closing phase. What is the project manager's response?

    a. Implement the changes to satisfy the stakeholder.

    b. Assess the impact on the project closure and discuss it with stakeholders.

    c. Reject the stakeholder request to maintain the integrity of the final report.

    d. Implement the changes without consulting the project team.

    Answer: c. Reject the stakeholder request to maintain the integrity of the final report.

11. **Scenario:** The project manager discovers that some project risks were not properly closed during the closing phase. What is the next step?

    a. Ignore the outstanding risks, assuming they are not critical for closure.

    b. Initiate the closure of the remaining risks to complete the project closure.

    c. Delay the project closure until all outstanding risks are resolved.

    d. Inform only senior management about the outstanding risks.

    Answer: b. Initiate the closure of the remaining risks to complete the project closure.

12. **Scenario:** The client requests additional project documentation after initiating the closure phase. What is the appropriate response?

a. Provide the requested documentation without further analysis.

b. Assess the need for additional documentation and discuss it with the client.

c. Reject the client's request, stating that closure processes are already in progress.

d. Delay providing the documentation to maintain control over project information.

Answer: b. Assess the need for additional documentation and discuss it with the client.

13. **Scenario:** Team members express concerns about the closure process, stating that it is rushed. What should the project manager do?

a. Ignore the team's concerns and proceed with closure as planned.

b. Review the closure process timeline and make necessary adjustments.

c. Delay the project closure until the team is comfortable with the process.

d. Conceal the team's concerns to maintain a positive image.

Answer: b. Review the closure process timeline and make necessary adjustments.

14. **Scenario:** The project manager realizes that some project expenses were not properly categorized in the financial closure. What is the immediate action?

a. Conceal the oversight to avoid financial scrutiny.

b. Amend the financial closure documents to include the proper categorization.

c. Seek legal advice before addressing the financial oversight.

d. Delay the financial closure until all expenses are properly categorized.

Answer: b. Amend the financial closure documents to include the proper categorization.

15. **Scenario:** The project manager receives requests for additional training during the closure phase. What is the project manager's response?

a. Disregard the training requests, assuming the team is already trained adequately.

b. Provide the necessary training to address identified skill gaps.

c. Delay the training until the next project phase.

d. Reject the training requests to avoid investing in additional resources.

Answer: b. Provide the necessary training to address identified skill gaps.

16. **Scenario:** A stakeholder requests changes to the final project budget during the closure phase. What is the project manager's response?

a. Implement the changes to satisfy the stakeholder.

b. Assess the impact on the project closure and discuss it with stakeholders.

c. Reject the stakeholder request to maintain the integrity of the final budget.

d. Implement the changes without consulting the project team.

Answer: c. Reject the stakeholder request to maintain the integrity of the final budget.

17. **Scenario:** The project manager discovers that some project activities were not properly closed during the closing phase. What is the next step?

a. Ignore the outstanding activities, assuming they are not critical for closure.

b. Initiate the closure of the remaining activities to complete the project closure.

c. Delay the project closure until all outstanding activities are resolved.

d. Inform only senior management about the outstanding activities.

Answer: b. Initiate the closure of the remaining activities to complete the project closure.

18. **Scenario:** Stakeholders express concerns about the project's environmental impact during the closure phase. What is the project manager's response?

a. Ignore the environmental concerns, assuming they are not relevant for closure.

b. Document the stakeholders' concerns and initiate corrective actions.

    c. Delay the project closure until all environmental concerns are addressed.

    d. Conceal the environmental concerns to maintain a positive image.

    Answer: b. Document the stakeholders' concerns and initiate corrective actions.

19. **Scenario:** The project manager discovers that some project risks were not properly documented during the closing phase. What is the next step?

    a. Ignore the documentation oversight, assuming it won't affect the overall project closure.

    b. Document the remaining risks and initiate the closure process.

    c. Delay the project closure until all risks are properly documented.

    d. Inform only senior management about the documentation oversight.

    Answer: b. Document the remaining risks and initiate the closure process.

20. **Scenario:** The project manager receives feedback from team members about the need for better communication during the closure phase. What is the appropriate response?

    a. Ignore the feedback, assuming communication is not critical for closure.

    b. Document the feedback and implement improvements in the communication process.

    c. Delay the project closure until all communication concerns are addressed.

    d. Conceal the communication feedback to avoid a negative image.

    Answer: b. Document the feedback and implement improvements in the communication process.

CHAPTER 3

Standard for Project Management

12 Principles[20] a Project manager should follow according to PMBOK 7. *Tip: This is important for answering PM mindset and scenario-based questions in the examination.*

1. **Be a diligent, respectful, and caring steward**
   - **Description:** Project managers should responsibly manage resources, respect stakeholders, and show care for the project's success.
   - **Example:** Ensuring that project resources are used efficiently and ethically and communicating respectfully with team members.

2. **Create a collaborative project team environment**
   - **Description:** Foster an environment where team members collaborate, communicate, and work together effectively.
   - **Example:** Organizing regular team meetings, encouraging open communication, and promoting a culture of collaboration.

3. **Effectively engage with stakeholders**
   - **Description:** Involve stakeholders appropriately throughout the project lifecycle.
   - **Example:** Regularly communicating project updates to stakeholders, seeking their input, and addressing their concerns.

4. **Focus on value**
   - **Description:** Concentrate efforts on delivering value to stakeholders and aligning project activities with organizational goals.

- **Example:** Prioritizing features that provide the most significant business value and aligning project goals with the organization's strategic objectives.

5. **Recognize, evaluate, and respond to system interactions**
   - **Description:** Consider the interconnectedness of various project elements and respond to interactions effectively.
   - **Example:** Understanding how changes in one part of the project might impact other areas and proactively managing those interactions.

6. **Demonstrate leadership behaviors**
   - **Description:** Exhibit leadership qualities, including motivation, inspiration, and guiding the team toward project success.
   - **Example:** Leading by example, motivating team members during challenging times, and providing clear direction.

7. **Tailor based on context**
   - **Description:** Adapt project management processes and practices based on the unique characteristics of the project and its environment.
   - **Example:** Choosing an agile or traditional approach depending on the nature of the project and the organization's culture.

8. **Build quality into processes and deliverables**
   - **Description:** Integrate quality assurance into all aspects of the project to ensure that processes and deliverables meet or exceed expectations.
   - **Example:** Implementing rigorous testing procedures to catch and address defects early in the project lifecycle.

9. **Navigate complexity**
   - **Description:** Effectively manage and navigate complexities inherent in projects.
   - **Example:** Using sophisticated project management techniques to handle intricate project structures or dealing with projects involving multiple stakeholders.

10. **Optimize risk responses**
   - **Description:** Continuously assess, respond to, and manage project risks to maximize positive outcomes.
   - **Example:** Developing contingency plans for identified risks and adjusting project plans based on evolving risk scenarios.
11. **Embrace adaptability and resiliency**
   - **Description:** Be open to change, adapt plans as necessary, and build resilience to overcome challenges.
   - **Example:** Quickly adjusting project timelines or strategies in response to unexpected changes in project requirements.
12. **Enable change to achieve the envisioned future state**
   - **Description:** Facilitate and manage change to reach the desired future state of the project.
   - **Example:** Implementing change management[14] strategies to ensure a smooth transition when introducing new processes or technologies.

3.1 Types of Leadership

1. **Autocratic Leadership[20]**
   - **Description:** The leader makes decisions without seeking input from others. It is a directive and controlling style.
   - **Example:** A military commander giving orders during a critical operation.
2. **Democratic Leadership**
   - **Description:** Decision making involves input from team members. The leader encourages participation and collaboration.
   - **Example:** A project manager facilitating a team discussion to reach a consensus on project goals.
3. **Transformational Leadership**
   - **Description:** Leaders inspire and motivate their teams to achieve extraordinary results. They focus on personal development and growth.
   - **Example:** A CEO who inspires employees to embrace innovation and take risks.

4. **Transactional Leadership**
   - **Description:** Leaders use reward and punishments to manage their teams. It involves clear expectations and consequences.
   - **Example:** A manager providing bonuses for achieving specific sales targets.

5. **Charismatic Leadership**
   - **Description:** Leaders influence others through their charisma, charm, and personal appeal.
   - **Example:** A political leader who captivates the audience with their speeches and vision.

6. **Servant Leadership**
   - **Description:** Leaders prioritize serving the needs of their team members. They focus on supporting and developing others.
   - **Example:** A team leader who actively seeks ways to help team members succeed.

7. **Laissez-Faire Leadership**
   - **Description:** Leaders adopt a hands-off approach, providing minimal guidance. It allows team members to make decisions independently.
   - **Example:** A manager allowing a team of experienced professionals to manage their projects.

8. **Situational Leadership**
   - **Description:** Leadership style adapts to the specific situation. The leader assesses the readiness of the team and adjusts their approach accordingly.
   - **Example:** A team lead switching between a more directive style for new team members and a more supportive style for experienced members.

9. **Strategic Leadership**
   - **Description:** Leaders focus on the long-term vision and strategy of the organization. They make decisions that align with the overall goals.

- **Example:** A CEO making decisions that position the company for future success in a changing market.

10. **Adaptive Leadership**
    - **Description:** Leaders navigate and thrive in complex and changing environments. They encourage adaptability and resilience.
    - **Example:** Leading a team through a major organizational change, such as a merger or restructuring.

Leadership skills include establishing a vision, critical reasoning, conflict management, and motivating team members.

Types of Motivation

1. **Intrinsic Motivation**
   - **Definition:** Internal drive that comes from within an individual.
   - **Example:** Pursuing a hobby for the sheer joy and satisfaction it brings.
2. **Extrinsic Motivation:**
   - **Definition:** External factors or rewards drive behavior.
   - **Example:** Working hard to receive a bonus or promotion.

Table 3.1 Concepts of reasoning[20]

Concept	Description
Critical Reasoning	Involves analyzing, evaluating, and forming well-reasoned judgments or decisions. It requires logical thinking, consideration of evidence, and assessing the validity of arguments.
Deductive Reasoning	A logical process where conclusions are derived from general principles or accepted premises. It guarantees a true conclusion if the premises are true. Involves moving from general to specific.
Inductive Reasoning	The process of making generalizations or forming theories based on specific observations or evidence. It suggests likely conclusions but doesn't guarantee absolute certainty.

Things That Impact Tailoring Leadership Styles

1. **Organizational Culture:**[20] The culture of the organization influences the leadership style that is most effective. A hierarchical culture may respond better to authoritative leadership, while a collaborative culture might favor a participative approach.

2. **Team Dynamics:** The composition, skills, and dynamics of the team can impact leadership style. Diverse teams or teams with high expertise may benefit from a more collaborative or transformational leadership style.

3. **Project Complexity:** The complexity of the project can influence the leadership style needed. A more transformational or adaptive leadership style might be necessary for complex projects.

4. **Project Phase:** The project life cycle phase can also impact leadership. In the early stages, a more directive approach may be needed, while in later stages, a delegative or coaching style might be more effective.

5. **Stakeholder Expectations:** Understanding the expectations and preferences of stakeholders is crucial. Tailoring leadership to align with stakeholder expectations ensures better communication and cooperation.

6. **Team Member Experience:** The experience level of team members is a significant factor. Novice team members may require more guidance and direction, while experienced professionals may thrive under a more hands-off leadership style.

7. **Crisis[4] or Change Situations:** During times of crisis or significant change, a more directive and authoritative leadership style might be necessary to provide clarity and stability.

8. **Individual Preferences:** Recognizing team members' individual preferences and strengths is essential. Tailoring leadership styles to match individual needs fosters better engagement and productivity.

9. **Cultural Diversity:** In globally diverse teams, cultural nuances play a role. A leader should be aware of cultural differences and adjust their style to accommodate various cultural expectations.

10. **Communication Channels:** The chosen communication channels and preferences of the team impact leadership styles. Some teams prefer regular face-to-face interactions, while others thrive in a virtual environment.

3.2 Difference Between Push and Pull Communication

Table 3.2 Differences between Push/Pull Communication[20]

Aspect	Push Communication	Pull Communication
Definition	Information is actively sent or "pushed" to recipients.	Information is made available, and recipients can access it when needed.
Initiative	Sender takes the initiative to share information.	Recipients take the initiative to seek information when needed.
Delivery	Through channels like e-mails, newsletters, announcements, and so on	Stored in accessible locations like shared databases or repositories.
Control	Sender has more control over timing and content.	Recipients have more control over when and what information they access.
Example	Project manager sending regular status updates to the team.	Providing project documentation in a shared folder.

3.3 Development Approach and Life Cycle {CADENCE}

The term "CADENCE"[20] in the context of the development approach and life cycle usually refers to a rhythmic pattern or flow, outlining the regularity and order of activities within a process. "CADENCE" can be associated with iterative and incremental development methodologies in software development and project management. Below is an explanation of how CADENCE might relate to development approaches and life cycles:

1. **Iterative Development**
   - **Explanation:** Iterative development involves breaking down the project into smaller cycles or iterations. Each iteration represents a complete development cycle, including planning, design, coding, testing, and deployment.
   - **CADENCE Connection:** The CADENCE here is the regular repetition of these iterations. Teams work through cycles with a consistent rhythm, continually refining and enhancing the product after each iteration.

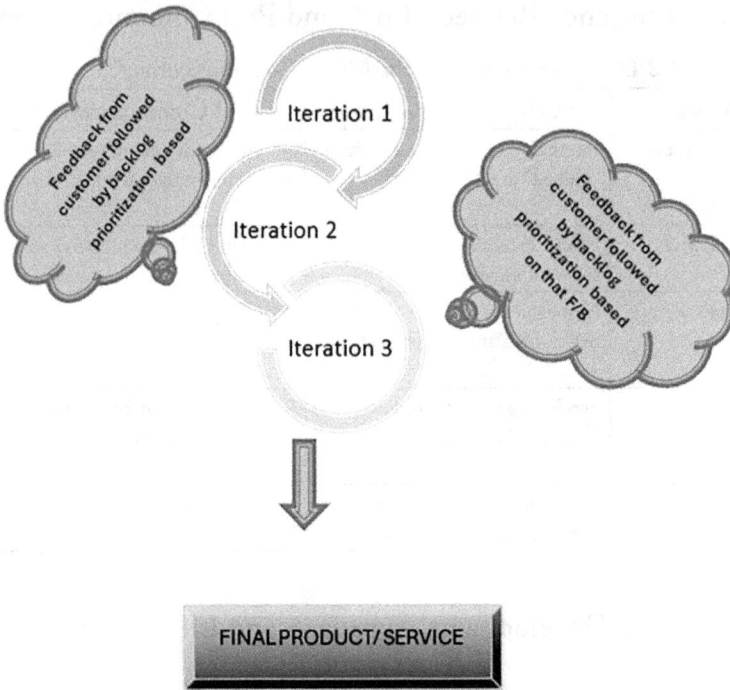

Figure 3.1 Iterative[20] approach

2. **Incremental Development**
   - **Explanation:** Incremental development involves building and delivering the software in small, incremental parts. Each increment adds new features or functionalities to the existing system.
   - **CADENCE Connection:** The CADENCE is reflected in the regular delivery of these increments. The team maintains a steady pace of delivering functional increments, allowing stakeholders to see progress regularly.

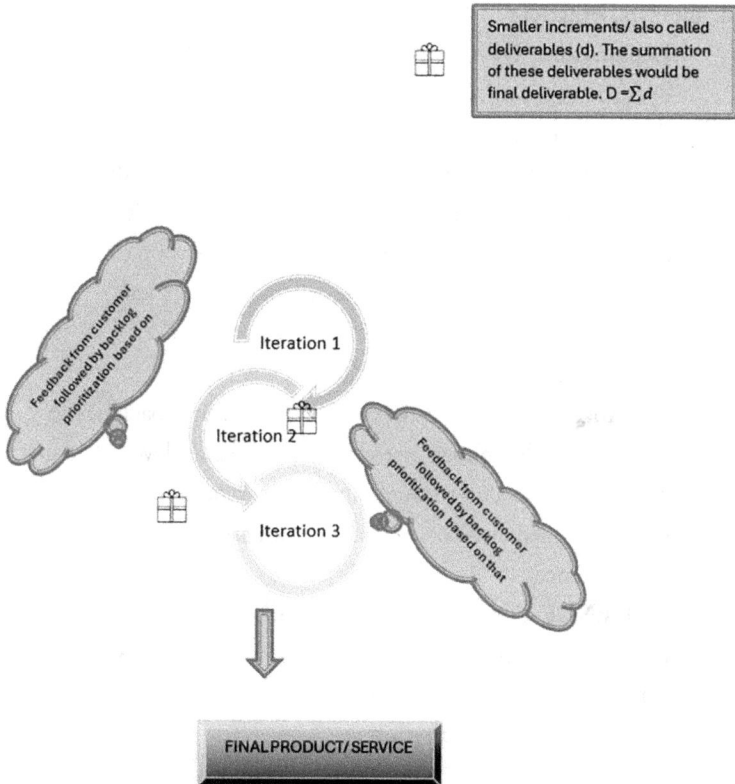

Smaller increments/ also called deliverables (d). The summation of these deliverables would be final deliverable. $D = \sum d$

Figure 3.2 Incremental[20] approach

3. Agile[20] Methodologies

- **Explanation:** Agile[25] methodologies, such as Scrum, emphasize iterative and incremental development. They promote adaptive planning, evolutionary development, and continuous improvement.
- **CADENCE Connection:** In Scrum, for example, there is a regular cadence of events, including sprint planning, daily stand-ups, sprint reviews, and retrospectives. The fixed-duration sprints create a predictable and rhythmic development cycle.

4. DevOps Practices

- **Explanation:** DevOps integrates development and operations, emphasizing collaboration and automation throughout the software development life cycle (SDLC).
- **CADENCE Connection:** Continuous integration, delivery, and deployment practices in DevOps create a consistent cadence of building, testing, and releasing software changes. This regular flow ensures a more reliable and efficient development process.

5. Waterfall[20] Model

- **Explanation:** While less flexible than Agile approaches, the waterfall model follows a sequential and linear development process, progressing through phases like requirements, design, implementation, testing, deployment, and maintenance.
- **CADENCE Connection:** The CADENCE in a waterfall model is more structured, with each phase having a specific time frame and set of activities. The flow is less iterative but follows a predictable rhythm.

In summary, CADENCE in the context of development approaches and life cycles often refers to the regular and rhythmic pattern of activities within iterative, incremental, or Agile methodologies. It ensures a predictable and sustainable pace for development teams.

The "FDBTDC" life cycle phases represent a sequence of key stages in a project or product development life cycle. Each phase has a specific purpose and set of activities. Here's an explanation of each phase[20]:

1. Feasibility (F)

- **Purpose:** Evaluate the viability of the project or product. Assess whether it is feasible in terms of technical, economic, legal, operational, and scheduling aspects.
- **Activities:** Conduct a feasibility study, define project goals, assess risks, and determine if the project aligns with organizational objectives.

2. **Design (D)**
   - **Purpose:** Develop detailed specifications for the project or product based on the findings from the feasibility phase. Create a blueprint that guides the development process.
   - **Activities:** Create system architecture, detailed specifications, design prototypes, and define the technical and functional aspects of the project.

3. **Build (B)**
   - **Purpose:** Implement the design specifications developed in the previous phase. This phase involves actual construction or development work.
   - **Activities:** Write code, create software, manufacture products, or build the project according to the design specifications.

4. **Test (T)**
   - **Purpose:** Evaluate the project or product to ensure that it meets the specified requirements and functions as intended.
   - **Activities:** Conduct various testing processes, including unit testing, integration testing, system testing, and user acceptance testing, to identify and rectify defects.

5. **Deploy (D)**
   - **Purpose:** Release the finalized project or product to the intended users or market. Ensure a smooth transition from the development environment to the operational environment.
   - **Activities:** Implement the product or project in the live environment, provide training to end-users, and address any deployment-related issues.

6. **Close (C)**
   - **Purpose:** Officially conclude the project or product development life cycle. This phase involves finalizing documentation, conducting project reviews, and transitioning responsibilities.
   - **Activities:** Document the project's outcomes, perform a project review or retrospective, close contracts, release resources, and transfer knowledge to maintenance or support teams.

These phases follow a sequential order, and each phase's outputs serve as inputs to the subsequent phase. The FDBTDC life cycle is a structured approach that helps manage and control the progression of a project or product from conceptualization to closure.

3.4 How Is Planning Strongly Related to the Development Approach?

Planning is strongly related to the development approach as it serves as the foundation for guiding the entire project or product development process. The planning phase is crucial in defining the goals, scope, timelines, and resource requirements. The connection between planning and development approach can be explained in several ways:

1. **Setting the Direction**
   - **Planning:** In the planning phase, the project objectives, requirements, and constraints are identified. This includes defining the scope, creating a schedule, and allocating resources.
   - **Development Approach:** The chosen development approach aligns with the project's goals. Whether it's an agile, waterfall, iterative, or other approach, it must be compatible with the project's scope and objectives.
2. **Resource Allocation**
   - **Planning:** Resource planning involves allocating personnel, budget, and equipment to specific tasks and activities. It helps in determining the skill sets required for the development.
   - **Development Approach:** The development approach influences resource allocation. For example, an agile approach may require cross-functional teams, while a waterfall approach may allocate resources differently.
3. **Risk Management**
   - **Planning:** Risk assessment and management planning are essential in the planning phase to identify potential challenges and develop strategies to mitigate or respond to risks.

- **Development Approach:** Different development approaches handle risks in distinct ways. Agile approaches, for instance, embrace change and manage risks iteratively, while waterfall aims for a comprehensive risk assessment upfront.

4. **Timeline and Milestones**
- **Planning:** The planning phase includes creating a timeline with milestones and deadlines. It sets the schedule for development activities.
- **Development Approach:** The development approach impacts the project timeline. With its iterative cycles, Agile may have more frequent milestones, while a waterfall approach may have fewer but larger milestones.

5. **Communication and Collaboration**
- **Planning:** Establishing communication channels and collaboration methods is part of the planning phase. It ensures that teams can effectively work together.
- **Development Approach:** The chosen development approach dictates how teams communicate and collaborate. Agile emphasizes regular communication and collaboration, while waterfall may have more structured and formalized communication.

In summary, planning serves as the roadmap for the development approach. The two are interconnected, with planning influencing the choice of development approach and the development approach shaping how the plan is executed. A well-defined plan ensures that the development approach is applied cohesively and effectively throughout the project life cycle.

3.5 System for Value Delivery

The "system for value delivery"[20] in project management typically refers to the structured and organized approach a project team employs to deliver maximum value to stakeholders. It encompasses various processes, methodologies, and practices designed to ensure that the project's outcomes align with the overall objectives and expectations. Here are the key components of a system for value delivery in project management:

1. **Project Management Methodology**[20]
   - Adopting a project management methodology, such as Agile, Scrum, or Waterfall, that aligns with the project's nature and requirements.
2. **Stakeholder Engagement**
   - Actively involving and engaging stakeholders throughout the project to understand their needs, expectations, and concerns.
3. **Requirements Management**
   - Implementing effective processes for gathering, documenting, and managing project requirements to ensure alignment with stakeholder expectations.
4. **Prioritization**[20]
   - Employing methods to prioritize project tasks and features based on their importance and impact on achieving project goals.
5. **Iterative Planning and Execution**
   - Breaking the project into manageable iterations or sprints, allowing for continuous reassessment and adjustment based on feedback and changing circumstances.
6. **Continuous Improvement**[20]
   - Implementing a culture of continuous improvement, where the team regularly reflects on its performance, identifies areas for enhancement, and implements changes.
7. **Risk Management**
   - Identifying, assessing, and managing risks throughout the project life cycle to minimize potential negative impacts on value delivery.
8. **Value Stream Mapping**
   - Analyzing and optimizing the value stream, visualizing how value is delivered from initiation to project completion.
9. **Metrics and Key Performance Indicators (KPIs)**
   - Establishing relevant metrics and KPIs to measure project progress, quality, and overall value delivery.
10. **Feedback Loops**[25]
    - Incorporating mechanisms for regular feedback from stakeholders and team members to adjust project activities and deliverables based on real-time insights.

11. **Change Management**
    - Implementing effective change management processes to handle alterations in project scope or requirements while ensuring continued value delivery. Case Study[14] from HBS regarding Leading Change at Harley-Davidson[14] helps examine leadership challenges during an organizational change initiative.

12. **Quality Assurance and Control**
    - Integrating robust processes for quality assurance and control to ensure that project deliverables meet or exceed predefined quality standards.

13. **Transparency and Communication**
    - Maintaining open and transparent communication channels to keep stakeholders informed about project progress, challenges, and achievements.

3.6 Questions for Practice

1. What does a project management methodology help achieve?
   a. Stakeholder engagement
   b. Continuous improvement
   c. Requirements management
   d. Structured approach to project activities

2. Why is stakeholder engagement crucial in project management?
   a. To prioritize tasks
   b. To gather and manage requirements
   c. To understand needs and expectations
   d. To implement a project methodology

3. What does value stream mapping aim to visualize?
   a. Project iterations
   b. Stakeholder expectations
   c. Delivery of value throughout the project
   d. Risk management processes

4. What is the purpose of continuous improvement in project management?
   a. To finalize project deliverables
   b. To identify areas for enhancement

      c. To establish project KPIs

      d. To implement change management

5. What does risk management involve in project management?

      a. Breaking the project into iterations

      b. Minimizing potential negative impacts

      c. Gathering and managing requirements

      d. Establishing quality standards

6. How do iterative planning and execution benefit value delivery?

      a. By finalizing project scope early

      b. By allowing for continuous reassessment

      c. By avoiding stakeholder engagement

      d. By implementing a one-time planning approach

7. Why are metrics and KPIs important in project management?

      a. To avoid continuous improvement

      b. To measure project progress and quality

      c. To exclude stakeholders from the process

      d. To decrease transparency

8. What is the primary goal of change management in project management?

      a. To avoid project iterations

      b. To implement a project methodology

      c. To handle alterations in project scope or requirements

      d. To minimize stakeholder engagement

9. How does quality assurance contribute to value delivery?

      a. By implementing change management

      b. By minimizing potential negative impacts

      c. By ensuring project deliverables meet predefined quality standards

      d. By excluding stakeholders from the process

10. What does transparency in project management involve?

      a. Keeping stakeholders informed about project progress

      b. Avoiding feedback loops

      c. Minimizing stakeholder engagement

      d. Implementing a one-time planning approach

Answers

1. **b. Continuous improvement**
   - A project management methodology helps achieve a structured approach to project activities, and continuous improvement is a key aspect.

2. **c. To understand needs and expectations**
   - Stakeholder engagement in project management is crucial to understanding the needs and expectations of the stakeholders.

3. **c. Delivery of value throughout the project**
   - Value stream mapping aims to visualize and improve the delivery of value throughout the entire project.

4. **b. To identify areas for enhancement**
   - The purpose of continuous improvement in project management is to identify areas for enhancement and make iterative improvements.

5. **b. Minimizing potential negative impacts**
   - Risk management in project management involves identifying and minimizing potential negative impacts on the project.

6. **b. By allowing for continuous reassessment**
   - Iterative planning and execution benefit value delivery by allowing for continuous reassessment and adjustment.

7. **b. To measure project progress and quality**
   - Metrics and Key Performance Indicators (KPIs) are important in project management to measure project progress and quality.

8. **c. To handle alterations in project scope or requirements**
   - The primary goal of change management in project management is to handle alterations in project scope or requirements.

9. **c. By ensuring project deliverables meet predefined quality standards**
   - Quality assurance in project management contributes to value delivery by ensuring project deliverables meet predefined quality standards.

10. **a. Keeping stakeholders informed about project progress**
   • Transparency in project management involves keeping stakeholders informed about project progress.

3.6.1 Scenario-Based Questions

1. You are managing a software development project, and during a retrospective meeting, the team identifies an area for improvement in the development process. How would you apply the concept of continuous improvement to enhance the project's value delivery?
   a. Ignore the feedback, as the project is already in progress.
   b. Discuss the identified improvement with the team and implement changes in the next sprint.
   c. Document the feedback but wait until the project is completed to address it.
   d. Inform the stakeholders about the identified improvement without taking any action.

2. In a construction project, you discover that a key stakeholder's expectations have changed. How would you handle this situation to ensure continued stakeholder satisfaction and value delivery?
   a. Proceed with the original plan, as changing stakeholder expectations are common.
   b. Update the project plan without informing the stakeholders.
   c. Engage with the stakeholders to understand the new expectations and adjust the project accordingly.
   d. Ignore the stakeholder's new expectations to avoid project delays.

3. Midway through a marketing campaign project, the client requests a significant change in the campaign strategy. How would you approach change management to ensure successful value delivery?
   a. Reject the change request to maintain the project's original scope.
   b. Implement the change without assessing its impact on the project.
   c. Evaluate the impact of the change, communicate it to the stakeholders, and implement it if feasible.
   d. Accept the change request without considering its consequences.

Answers: 1b, 2c, 3c

3.7 Tailoring

Tailoring refers to customizing or adapting project management processes, methodologies, and documentation to better suit a particular project's specific needs and characteristics. It involves making deliberate choices about which project management processes and elements are applied, modified, or excluded based on the project's unique requirements.

Tailoring is essential because every project is unique, and applying a one-size-fits-all approach may not be effective. It allows project managers to strike a balance between following established best practices and meeting the project's and its stakeholders' specific needs. Tailoring is often guided by organizational policies, industry standards, and the principles outlined in project management frameworks like the Project Management Body of Knowledge[20] (PMBOK) or Agile methodologies.

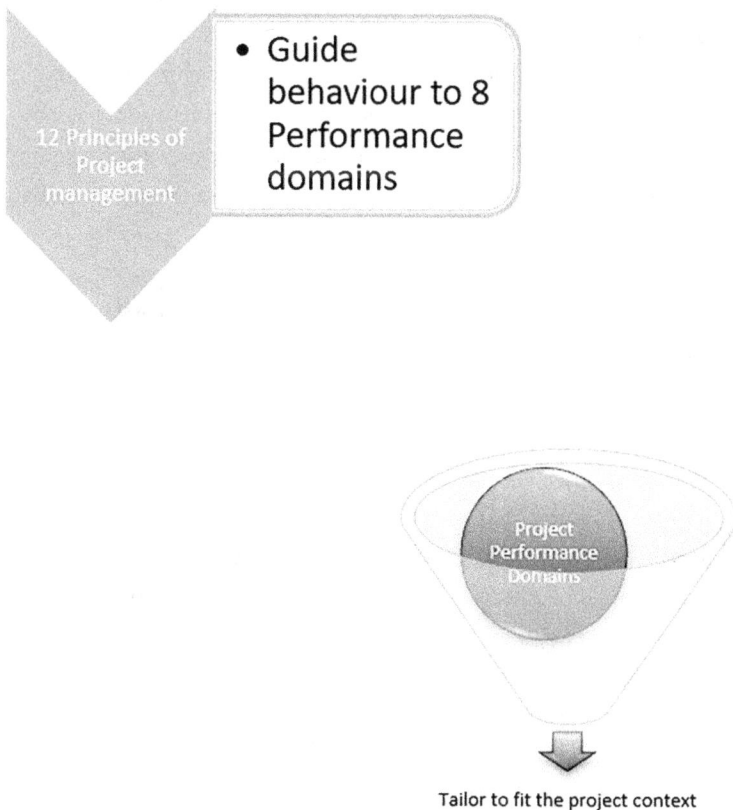

Figure 3.3 Tailoring[20]

3.8 Project Performance Domain

One commonly recognized framework that defines project performance domains is the Talent Triangle[20] introduced by the Project Management Institute[20] (PMI). The Talent Triangle identifies three key skill areas or domains essential for project professionals:

1. Technical Project Management: This domain encompasses the foundational project management skills and knowledge required to manage projects effectively. It includes expertise in project planning, scope management, scheduling, budgeting, risk management, and other technical aspects of project delivery.
2. Leadership:[20] The leadership domain focuses on the interpersonal and leadership skills needed to guide and motivate project teams. Effective communication, team building, conflict resolution, and the ability to influence stakeholders are critical components of this domain.
3. Strategic and Business Management: This domain emphasizes the alignment of projects with organizational goals and strategic objectives. Project professionals need to understand the business context, make strategic decisions, and contribute to the overall success and value of the organization.

These three domains collectively form the Talent Triangle, reflecting a holistic view of the skills required for successful project management. PMI encourages project professionals to develop competencies in each domain to enhance their ability to manage projects effectively and contribute to organizational success.

It's important to note that specific frameworks or models used in project management may have different ways of categorizing or naming performance domains. Always refer to the specific guidelines or frameworks applicable to your context for accurate information.

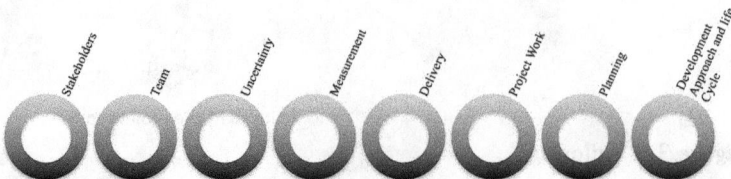

Figure 3.4 Performance domains[20]

1. **Tailoring for Uncertainty**

   Description: Tailoring for uncertainty involves adapting project management processes to the level of uncertainty in a project. This ensures appropriate risk management and flexibility are incorporated into the project plan.

   Scenario-Based Example: In a software development project where technology advancements may introduce uncertainties, tailoring would involve implementing agile practices for adaptive planning and continuous reassessment of requirements.

   Just to refresh types of uncertainty: PESTLE

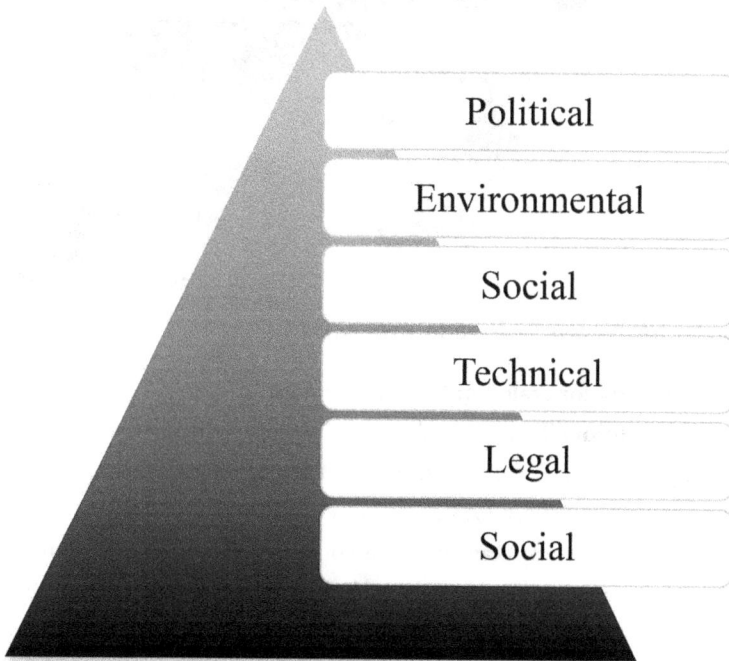

Figure 3.5 Types of uncertainty

How to respond to Ambiguity?[20]

- Use Progressive elaboration/experimenting/prototyping.

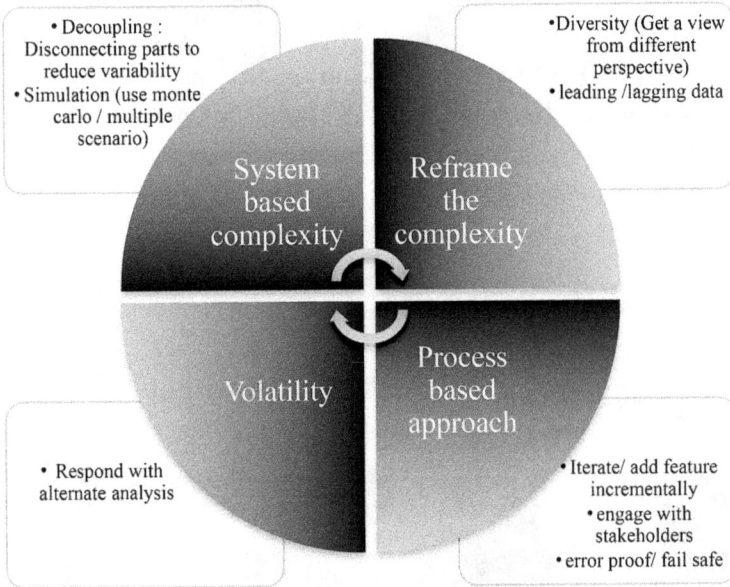

Figure 3.6 Ways to respond to ambiguity

2. **Tailoring for Stakeholder Management**

   Description: Tailoring stakeholder management involves customizing communication and engagement strategies to meet the needs and expectations of diverse stakeholders.

   Scenario-Based Example: In a construction project with multiple stakeholders, tailoring might include employing varied communication channels such as regular progress reports for investors, town hall meetings for the local community, and detailed technical briefings for engineers.

3. **Tailoring for Team Management**

   Description: Tailoring for team management involves adjusting leadership and collaboration approaches based on the characteristics and dynamics of the project team.

   Scenario-Based Example: In a global project with a culturally diverse team, tailoring would involve incorporating cross-cultural training, fostering open communication channels, and leveraging virtual collaboration tools to bridge geographical gaps.

4. **Tailoring Development Approach**

   Description: Tailoring the development approach involves selecting an appropriate methodology or combination of methodologies based on the nature of the project, organizational culture, and specific requirements.

   Scenario-Based Example: For a research and development project with evolving requirements, tailoring might involve adopting a hybrid approach that combines elements of agile and traditional project management methodologies to balance adaptability with structured planning.

5. **Tailoring for Life Cycle Planning**

   Description: Tailoring life cycle planning involves choosing an appropriate project life cycle model (e.g., predictive, iterative, incremental) based on project characteristics and objectives.

   Scenario-Based Example: In a construction project where requirements are well-defined upfront, tailoring may involve selecting a predictive life cycle model, such as the Waterfall model, to ensure a systematic and controlled progression through stages.

6. **Tailoring for Project Work Delivery Measurement**

   Description: Tailoring project work delivery measurement involves defining key performance indicators (KPIs) and measurement criteria aligned with project goals.

   Scenario-Based Example: In an infrastructure project focused on on-time delivery, tailoring would involve setting KPIs related to milestones and completion timelines, with regular performance reviews and adjustments to the plan as needed.

7. **Tailoring for Planning Project Work**

   Description: Tailoring for planning project work involves adjusting planning processes to the project's size, complexity, and requirements, ensuring that planning is proportionate to the project's needs.

   Scenario-Based Example: In a small-scale project with relatively low complexity, tailoring would involve streamlining planning processes to avoid unnecessary documentation and bureaucracy while ensuring essential aspects are adequately addressed.

These tailored approaches help project managers and teams adapt to the unique characteristics of each project, maximizing the chances of success and delivering value to stakeholders.

3.9 Questions for Practice

1. What is a key consideration when tailoring the risk management plan for project uncertainty?
   A. Implementing generic risk strategies
   B. Adapting risk responses based on project-specific uncertainties
   C. Ignoring uncertainties for simplicity
   D. Avoiding risk assessments
   Answer: B. Adapting risk responses based on project-specific uncertainties

2. In tailoring stakeholder engagement strategies for a global project, what is a crucial aspect to consider?
   A. Implementing a standardized communication approach
   B. Adapting communication strategies to cultural nuances and stakeholder expectations
   C. Ignoring cultural differences for simplicity
   D. Limiting stakeholder involvement to avoid conflicts
   Answer: B. Adapting communication strategies to cultural nuances and stakeholder expectations

3. When tailoring leadership styles for a diverse team, what is a challenge project managers might face?
   A. Enforcing a single leadership approach for consistency
   B. Adapting to different team preferences and dynamics
   C. Ignoring team dynamics for simplicity
   D. Avoiding communication with team members
   Answer: B. Adapting to different team preferences and dynamics

4. What is the primary advantage of tailoring the development approach for each project?
   A. Maintaining a one-size-fits-all strategy for consistency
   B. Adapting to unique project needs and complexities
   C. Ignoring project complexities for simplicity
   D. Strictly adhering to traditional methods
   Answer: B. Adapting to unique project needs and complexities

5. How can tailoring the project life cycle contribute to better project outcomes?

A. Applying the same life cycle to all projects

B. Ignoring project-specific needs for simplicity

C. Adapting phases to align with project characteristics

D. Standardizing life cycle phases for consistency

Answer: C. Adapting phases to align with project characteristics

6. Why is tailoring performance measurement criteria crucial for project work delivery?

A. Applying uniform criteria for all projects

B. Ignoring performance measurement for simplicity

C. Adapting criteria to capture unique project aspects

D. Relying solely on subjective assessments

Answer: C. Adapting criteria to capture unique project aspects

7. In a project with a fixed budget, what challenges might project managers face when tailoring planning processes?

A. Ignoring budget constraints for flexibility

B. Adapting to changing requirements without constraints

C. Ensuring planning is rigid and inflexible

D. Customizing planning to fit budget constraints and changing requirements

Answer: D. Customizing planning to fit budget constraints and changing requirements

8. What role does tailoring play in managing uncertainties throughout the project life cycle?

A. Avoiding all uncertainties for simplicity

B. Adapting strategies to minimize the impact of uncertainties

C. Implementing generic risk responses

D. Ignoring uncertainties completely

Answer: B. Adapting strategies to minimize the impact of uncertainties

9. When tailoring stakeholder engagement for diverse projects, what challenges might project managers encounter?

A. Standardizing communication without considering cultural differences

B. Adapting communication strategies to cultural nuances

C. Ignoring cultural diversity for simplicity

D. Limiting stakeholder engagement to avoid conflicts

Answer: B. Adapting communication strategies to cultural nuances

10. What potential benefits can project managers derive from tailoring leadership styles in team management?

    A. Enforcing a single leadership style for consistency

    B. Adapting leadership to match team preferences and dynamics

    C. Ignoring team preferences for simplicity

    D. Avoiding leadership responsibilities

    Answer: B. Adapting leadership to match team preferences and dynamics

11. In a project with high uncertainties, what would be the most suitable tailoring approach for risk management?

    A. Implementing generic risk strategies

    B. Adapting risk responses based on project-specific uncertainties

    C. Avoiding risk assessments

    D. Ignoring uncertainties for simplicity

    Answer: B. Adapting risk responses based on project-specific uncertainties

12. You're managing a project with diverse stakeholders from different cultural backgrounds. How should you tailor your stakeholder engagement strategies?

    A. Standardizing communication without considering cultural differences

    B. Adapting communication strategies to cultural nuances

    C. Ignoring cultural diversity for simplicity

    D. Limiting stakeholder engagement to avoid conflicts

    Answer: B. Adapting communication strategies to cultural nuances

13. When leading a team with varying preferences and dynamics, which approach is most effective for tailoring leadership styles?

    A. Enforcing a single leadership style for consistency

    B. Adapting leadership to match team preferences and dynamics

    C. Ignoring team preferences for simplicity

    D. Avoiding leadership responsibilities

    Answer: B. Adapting leadership to match team preferences and dynamics

14. Match the tailoring concept with its description:

Table 3.3 Mix and match question

Tailoring Concept	Description
A. Development Approach Tailoring	Tailoring the project life cycle based on project characteristics
B. Life Cycle Planning Tailoring	Adapting performance measurement criteria to capture unique project aspects
C. Project Work Delivery Measurement Tailoring	Customizing planning processes to fit budget constraints and changing requirements
D. Planning Project Work Tailoring	Adapting the development approach to unique project needs and complexities

Table 3.4 Answer: Mix and match question

Tailoring Concept	Description
A. Development Approach Tailoring	Adapting the development approach to unique project needs and complexities
B. Life Cycle Planning Tailoring	Tailoring the project life cycle based on project characteristics
C. Project Work Delivery Measurement Tailoring	Adapting performance measurement criteria to capture unique project aspects
D. Planning Project Work Tailoring	Customizing planning processes to fit budget constraints and changing requirements

CHAPTER 4

Models/Methods/Artifacts

A Model[20] is a simplified representation or framework that captures essential aspects of a complex system, process, or phenomenon. It serves as a tool for understanding, analyzing, or predicting behaviors, interactions, or outcomes within a specific context.

4.1 Commonly Used Models

1. **Situational Leadership Model**
   - **Definition:** Situational Leadership is a leadership style framework developed by Paul Hersey[23] and Ken Blanchard (model measures competence, commitment), emphasizing the adaptability of leadership styles based on the readiness or maturity of followers. Others include OSCAR:[20] Outcome, Situation, Choices/Consequences, Actions, and Review.
   - **Key Components:** Four leadership styles – Directing, Coaching, Supporting, and Delegating, are applied based on the followers' competence and commitment levels.

2. **Communication[20] Model**
   - The message is influenced by the sender/receiver's current KELTC[20] Motivation Model: Knowledge, Experience, Language, Thinking, and Communication style.
   - Effectiveness of communication channel (Alistair[20] Cockburn) Richness, effectiveness
   - Gulf of execution and evaluation: Does it match what we expect to be done? Does it allow the user to discover how to interact with it? Donald Norman
   - Maslow's Hierarchy of Needs is a renowned motivational framework delineating the five tiers of human needs that impact behavior. These include physiological, safety, love and

belonging, esteem, and self-actualization needs, all serving as motivational forces.

3. **Model for Motivation**

- Herzberg's Two-Factor Theory:[20] Herzberg proposed that job satisfaction and dissatisfaction are influenced by different factors. Hygiene factors, such as salary and working conditions, mitigate dissatisfaction, whereas motivators, such as recognition and advancement, serve to inspire and drive individuals.
- Theory of Needs (McClelland): McClelland's theory suggests that individuals are motivated by three needs: achievement, affiliation, and power. Depending on which need is dominant, people are driven to seek different types of goals and rewards.[20]
- Intrinsic versus Extrinsic Motivation: Intrinsic motivation comes from within, driven by personal enjoyment or fulfillment from an activity. Extrinsic motivation, on the contrary, stems from external incentives or external pressures.[20]
- Theory X, Y, Z (Douglas McGregor): McGregor proposed two contrasting management styles in Theory X and Theory Y. Theory X assumes employees dislike work and need to be closely controlled and coerced. Theory Y posits that employees are inherently motivated and capable of self-direction. Theory Z expands on McGregor's theories by emphasizing long-term employment, collective decision-making, and a strong company culture.[20]

4. **Change Model**

- The ADKAR[20] Model (Awareness, Desire, Knowledge, Ability, Reinforcement) is commonly used for individual change management.
- FPISM: Formulate the change, Plan the change, Implement the change, Sustain the change, Manage the transition (to the new state).[20]
- John Kotter's[20] eight steps to change: Create Urgency, form a powerful coalition, create a vision for change, communicate

the change, remove obstacles, create short-term wins, build on the change, and anchor those changes in the corporate model.

- Virginia Satir Change[20] Model: Late Status Quo Business as usual: the initial stage when everything feels familiar), Foreign Element (Shift in Status Quo), Chaos (since people are in unfamiliar territory), Transforming Idea, Practice and Integration, New Status Quo.
- Transition Model: Ending, losing, and letting go, neutral zone, new beginning (William Bridges).

5. **Complexity Model**
- **Cynefin Framework** by Dave Snowden[20] categorizes problems into Simple, Complicated, Complex, and Chaotic domains, offering guidance on problem-solving approaches. If an obvious cause-effect relationship exists, use best practices to make decisions. If a complex relationship with **known unknowns**, then assess the facts and use good practices for **unknown-unknowns**: Probe the environment and iterate forwards. For a chaotic environment, stabilize the situation and take steps to reduce the complexity. For a disordered situation, break it into smaller parts, then assess.
- **Stacey Matrix**: Measures the uncertainty of the deliverable and technology to create it.

$$\begin{bmatrix} \text{simple} & \text{complicated} \\ \text{complex} & \text{chaotic} \end{bmatrix} = \textit{item characteristics that should be considered for measuring}$$

6. **Project Team Development Model**
- **Tuckman's Stages** of Group Development outlines the stages of forming, storming, norming, performing, and adjourning in team development.
- **Drexler/Sibbet:**[20] Orientation (why), Trust Building (who), Goal Clarification (what), Commitment (how), Implementation (Plans), High performance, Renewal.

4.2 Artifacts

An artifact[20] can be a template, document, or project deliverable. Types of artifacts include:

- Strategic: Like Business Case, Business Model Canvas, Project Brief, Project Charter, Product Roadmaps, Project Plan, Change Control Plan, Communication Management Plan, Cost Management, Iteration Plan, Procurement Management Plan, Resource Management Plan, Risk Management Plan, Scope Management Plan, Schedule Management Plan, Stakeholder Management Plan.
- Logs and Registers: Like Assumption Logs, Backlog, Risk Adjusted Backlog, Change Logs, Issue Logs, Lessons Learned Register, Stakeholder Register, and Risk Register.
- Charts like Control Charts, Hierarchy Charts, Organizational Breakdown Structures, Product Breakdown Structures, Resource Breakdown Structures, Risk Breakdown Structures, Work Breakdown Structures.
- Baseline documents like Budget, Milestone Schedule, Performance Measurement Baseline, Project Schedule, Scope Baseline, and so on.
- Visual data and information: Affinity Diagrams, Burn up/ Burn Down Charts, Cause and Effect Diagrams, CFD: Cumulative Flow Diagrams, Cycle Time Charts, Flow Charts, Lead Time Charts, Prioritization Matrix, Schedule Network Diagram, VSM, S-Curve, Use Cases, Velocity Charts, Reports (Quality, Risk), Agreements and Contracts, Resource Calendars.

CHAPTER 5

Agile Management

Agile Overview20: Agile[26] is a project management and product development approach that prioritizes flexibility, collaboration, and customer satisfaction. It emphasizes iterative and incremental delivery, allowing teams to respond quickly to changing requirements and deliver valuable products in shorter cycles. Agile[25] methodologies prioritize individuals and interactions, working solutions, and customer collaboration over strict processes and documentation.

Types of Agile Methodologies

1. **Scrum**[25]

   Key Concepts
   - Scrum Teams: Cross-functional teams working in fixed-length iterations (sprints)
   - Scrum Master: Facilitator of the Scrum process
   - Product Owner: Represents the customer and defines priorities

   Artifacts
   - Product Backlog: A prioritized list of features or tasks
   - Sprint Backlog: A subset of the product backlog for the current sprint
   - Increment: The sum of completed product backlog items

2. **Kanban**

   Key Concepts
   - Visual Board: Represents the workflow of tasks
   - Work in Progress (WIP) Limits: Controls the number of tasks in each stage

- Continuous Delivery: Focuses on a smooth, continuous flow of work

Artifacts

- Kanban Board: Visualizes tasks moving through stages (To Do, In Progress, Done)

3. **Extreme Programing[26] (XP)**

Key Practices

- Test-Driven Development (TDD): Writing tests before coding
- Continuous Integration: Frequent integration of code changes
- Pair Programing: Two programers working together at one workstation

Values

- Communication, simplicity, feedback, and courage

4. **Lean Software Development**

Key Principles

- Eliminate Waste: Remove unnecessary steps in the development process.
- Amplify Learning: Foster a culture of continuous improvement.
- Deliver as Fast as Possible: Aim for quick and incremental deliveries.

Terms Used in Agile[25] Management

1. **User Story**
   - A concise description of a feature told from the end user's perspective

2. **Sprint**
   - A time-boxed iteration of work in Scrum, usually 1–4 weeks long

3. **Backlog**
   - A prioritized list of tasks, features, or user stories to be worked on

4. **Retrospective**
   - A meeting is held at the end of each sprint to review and improve the team's processes

5. **Daily Standup (Daily Scrum)**
   - A brief daily meeting where team members share updates on their work

6. **Burndown[26] Chart**
   - A visual representation of work completed versus work remaining in a sprint

7. **Velocity[26]**
   - A measure of the amount of work a team can complete in a sprint

8. **Product Owner**
   - Represents the customer and defines priorities in Scrum

9. **Scrum[26] Master**
   - Facilitator of the Scrum process, supporting the team and ensuring adherence to Scrum practices

10. **Kanban Board**
    - Visualizes tasks moving through different stages of a workflow

11. **Continuous Integration**
    - Developers frequently integrate code changes, ensuring regular builds and tests.

12. **Pair Programing**
    - Two programers working together at one workstation

These terms contribute to creating a shared understanding and effective communication within Agile teams.

5.1 Quick Bites

1. SCRUM = Empiricism (Knowledge and Experience) + Lean[17] Thinking (Reduces wastes and focus on essentials)
2. Scrum Values = CORFC: Commitment, Focus, Openness, Respect, Courage
3. Pillars: TIA[25]→Transparency, Adaptation, Inspection
4. Scrum Artifacts: Product Backlog, Sprint Backlog, Increment

| Artifact: Product Backlog, Sprint Backlog, Increment | | Product Goal, Sprint Goal, Definition of Done |

Commitment

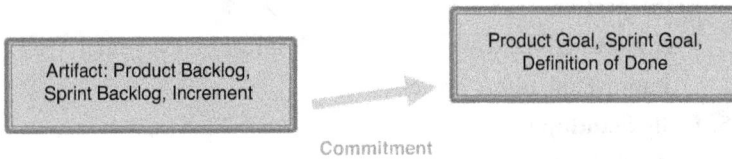

Figure 5.1 Artifact and product

5. Scrum[25] Events: Sprint, Sprint planning, Sprint Review, Sprint Retrospective, Daily Scrum

- The commencement of a new sprint occurs promptly upon the completion of the preceding sprint.
- Scope is subject to renegotiation.
- The Product Owner retains the authority to terminate a sprint if the established goal becomes obsolete.
- Sprint duration ranges from 2 to 4 weeks.
- A shorter sprint duration enhances the learning experience while concurrently reducing associated risks.
- The increment produced during a sprint must be usable, although deployment is not mandatory.

Sprint

Figure 5.2 Quick tips on sprint

- Time Box: 15 minutes (fixed)
- Not the only meeting of the day
- Developers conduct and choose an appropriate structure for the meeting.
- Typical structure involves addressing three questions:

Daily Scrum

- What needs to be done today?
- What was done in the last 24 hours?
- What should be planned for the next 24 hours, and are there any roadblocks.

- Meeting can be held at any time during the day, but it is recommended to schedule it as early as possible consistently at the same time every day.

Figure 5.3 Quick tips on daily scrum

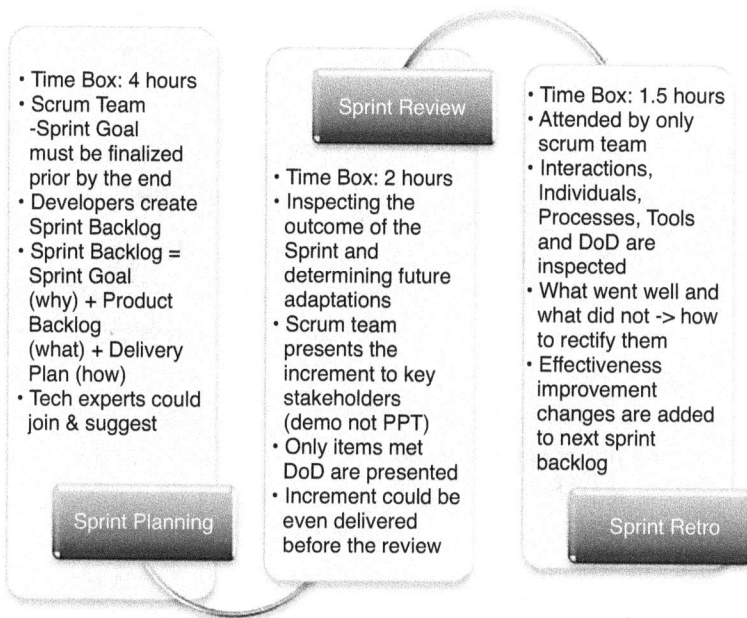

- Time Box: 4 hours
- Scrum Team
  -Sprint Goal
  must be finalized
  prior by the end
- Developers create
  Sprint Backlog
- Sprint Backlog =
  Sprint Goal
  (why) + Product
  Backlog
  (what) + Delivery
  Plan (how)
- Tech experts could
  join & suggest

Sprint Planning

Sprint Review

- Time Box: 2 hours
- Inspecting the
  outcome of the
  Sprint and
  determining future
  adaptations
- Scrum team
  presents the
  increment to key
  stakeholders
  (demo not PPT)
- Only items met
  DoD are presented
- Increment could be
  even delivered
  before the review

- Time Box: 1.5 hours
- Attended by only
  scrum team
- Interactions,
  Individuals,
  Processes, Tools
  and DoD are
  inspected
- What went well and
  what did not -> how
  to rectify them
- Effectiveness
  improvement
  changes are added
  to next sprint
  backlog

Sprint Retro

Figure 5.4 Quick tips on sprint planning, review, and retro

5.2 Types of Estimates: Agile versus Traditional Approach

1. **Flow-Based Estimates**[20]
   - **Definition:** Flow-based estimates[9] involve predicting the time
     it takes for work items to move through a system or process. It's
     based on analyzing the historical flow of similar work items.
   - **Unit:** Typically expressed in time units (e.g., hours and days)
     to complete a specific task or user story
   - **Focus:** Emphasizes the actual time taken for tasks to progress
     from start to finish
2. **Relative Estimating**
   - **Definition:** Relative estimating involves comparing the sizes
     or complexities of different work items. It's a comparative
     measure rather than an absolute time estimate.
   - **Unit:** Commonly uses abstract units such as story points or
     t-shirt sizes (small, medium, large) to represent the size or
     effort required for a task relative to others

- **Focus:** Concentrates on the relative effort or complexity of tasks compared to each other

5.2.1 Preference in Agile versus Adaptive versus Waterfall

1. **Agile**
   - **Flow-Based Estimates:** Agile methodologies often favor flow-based estimates, especially in frameworks like Kanban. The emphasis is on continuous delivery, and understanding the flow of work items is crucial.
   - **Relative Estimating:** Relative estimating, particularly in the form of story points, is also common in Agile, especially in Scrum. It allows teams to focus on the relative effort needed without being constrained by specific time units.
2. **Adaptive (Iterative Development)**
   - **Flow-Based Estimates:** Adaptive approaches involving iterative development may benefit from a combination of flow-based and relative estimates. Flow-based for understanding cycle times and relative for comparing the complexity of iterative increments.
   - **Relative Estimating:** Useful for adapting to changes and understanding the evolving complexity of the project.
3. **Waterfall**
   - **Flow-Based Estimates:** Waterfall projects often rely more on detailed flow-based estimates. Detailed planning is done upfront, and timelines are critical.
   - **Relative Estimating:** Less common in traditional waterfall models, as the focus is on a comprehensive upfront plan with specific time-based milestones.

Choosing the Best Approach

- **Agile:** A blend of both flow-based and relative estimating is common in agile methodologies. Teams often use flow metrics for continuous improvement and relative estimates for sprint planning.

- **Adaptive:** A flexible approach that may incorporate both types of estimates depending on the project's nature and requirements.
- **Waterfall:** Primarily relies on detailed flow-based estimates due to its sequential and plan-driven nature. The waterfall is usually best chosen when the scope is fixed, whereas agile is the best possibility when the time is fixed.

Ultimately, the choice depends on the project's characteristics, the need for adaptability, and the team's preferences and experience. Many agile teams find success in using a combination of both flow-based and relative estimating for a more comprehensive understanding of their work.

5.3 Burn-Up and Burn-Down Charts

A Burn-Up[19] chart illustrates the cumulative work completed over time, providing a visual representation of progress toward the project's total scope or goals. Here's a simplified example:

- **X-Axis (Horizontal):** Time (Sprints or Weeks) or number of iterations
- **Y-Axis (Vertical):** Amount of Work Completed

In this example, the triangle line represents the total work scope (e.g., user stories or story points). The diamond line shows the work expected, and the square refers to the actual work completed in each sprint. As sprints progress, the line moves upward, indicating the cumulative completion of tasks. The burn-up chart helps teams and stakeholders track progress and assess if the project is on track to meet its goals.

The triangle line indicates an increased slope as higher story points are added. During that time between iterations 7 and 8, the story points almost remain constant, and not much work is done.

Other reasons when you might see a similar graph are when the story points are complex, or maybe there was some other complexity where the scrum master wasn't able to remove the impediments timely or not enough resources are there to support the work, or the story points are not elaborate enough, or the estimation of stories are not realistic, or maybe the team just didn't fill in their completed stories yet. There can be multiple reasons for the velocity to get slower.

Note that we need the story points to be elaborate enough; it doesn't necessarily mean they have to be long.

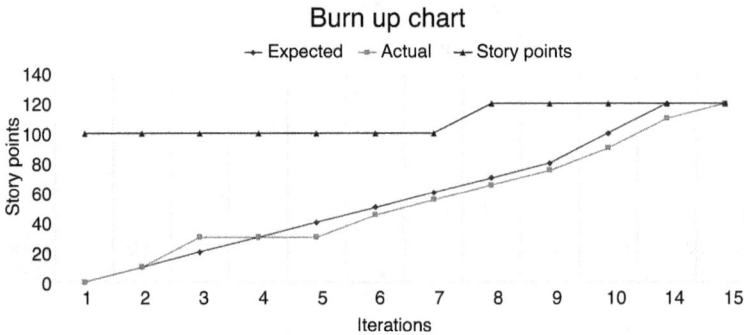

Figure 5.5 Burn-Up chart

Burn-Down Chart Example

A Burn-Down[20] chart illustrates the remaining work overtime, helping teams monitor their progress toward completing the planned work within a sprint or project. Here's a simplified example:

- **X-Axis (Horizontal):** Time (Sprints or Weeks)
- **Y-Axis (Vertical):** Remaining Work

In this example, as tasks are completed, the line moves downward. The Burn-Down chart provides a clear view of whether the team is on track to complete the work by the end of the project or sprint.

Both Burn-Up and Burn-Down charts are valuable tools for Agile teams to communicate progress transparently, identify trends, and make data-driven decisions throughout the project's lifecycle.

Figure 5.6 presents a Burn-Down chart comparing "actual" versus "desired" story points.

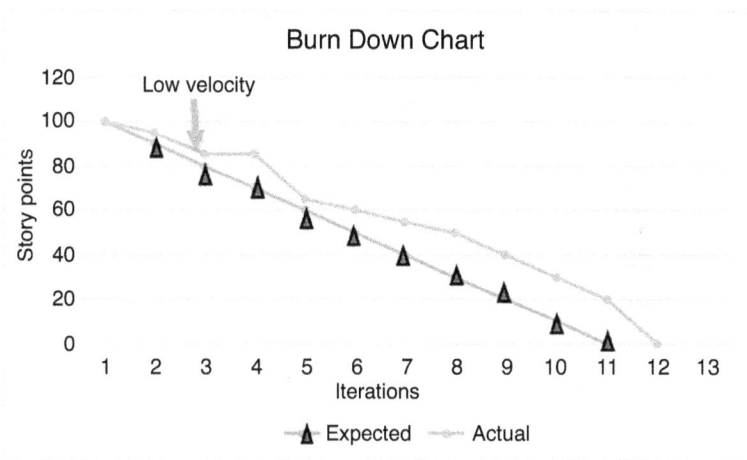

Figure 5.6 Burn-Down chart

The choice between using a Burn-Up chart or a Burn-Down chart depends on the specific needs and preferences of your project team and stakeholders. Both charts provide valuable insights into project progress, but they have distinct characteristics:

1. **Burn-Up Chart**
   Advantages
   - Shows the total amount of work planned for the project
   - Provides a clear indication of the scope of the project
   - Allows stakeholders to see if additional work has been added during the project

   Use Case
   - Suitable when there might be changes in scope and stakeholders want to visualize the cumulative work completed against the total planned work

2. **Burn-Down Chart**
   Advantages
   - Emphasizes the remaining work to be completed
   - Offers a clear indication of how well the team is progressing toward the goal

- Commonly used in Agile and Scrum methodologies

Use Case

- Suitable for projects where the focus is on completing the planned work within a fixed time frame and where scope changes are minimal

Considerations:

- **Project Nature:** The nature of your project and the level of detail you want to communicate might influence the choice between the two charts.
- **Stakeholder Preferences:** Some stakeholders might prefer one type of chart over the other based on their understanding and preferences.
- **Project Methodology:** Agile projects often lean toward burn-down charts, while projects with evolving scope may benefit from burn-up charts.

5.4 Scrum Team Members, Roles

Scrum Master True Leader

- **Role:** Scrum Master
- **Definition:** Servant-leader facilitating Scrum implementation.
- **Accountability:** Ensures adherence to Scrum principles.
- **Responsibilities:**
  - Facilitator and Coach
  - Obstacle Removal
  - Promoting Collaboration
  - Continuous Improvement
  - Shielding from External Interruptions
  - Servant Leadership
  - Understanding Scrum Principles
- **Focus:** Team facilitation, continuous improvement, and servant leadership.
- **Authority:** Facilitative, not authoritative.

Figure 5.7 Key points: Scrum master[25]

Developers/ Development team Self-organising, cross functional , DOD creation

- **Definition:** Team members responsible for creating the product increment.
- **Accountability:** Delivering the product increment during each Sprint.
- **Responsibilities:**
  - Collaborating on Sprint Planning
  - Actively participating in Daily Standups
  - Contributing to Sprint Review
  - Engaging in Sprint Retrospective
  - Writing and testing code
  - Ensuring code quality and adherence to Definition of Done
  - Collaborating with other team members and stakeholders
- **Focus:** Development tasks, code quality, and achieving Sprint goals.
- **Authority:** Shared responsibility within the development team. No hierarchical authority.
- Since they are cross functional, it's important that in agile, they self-learn through cross functional teams and T structure

Figure 5.8 Key points: Developers[25]

Product Owner Maximizing value of product

- **Definition:** Represents the stakeholders and ensures the Scrum Team delivers value.
- **Accountability:** Maximizing the value of the product and managing the Product Backlog.
- **Responsibilities:**
  - Creating and prioritizing the Product Backlog
  - Defining and communicating product goals and vision
  - Participating in Sprint Planning
  - Making decisions on product features and priorities
  - Available for the team to answer questions during development
  - Accepting or rejecting work results during Sprint Review
  - Adjusting priorities based on feedback and changes
- **Focus:** Value maximization, product vision, and effective communication with the team.
- **Authority:** Decision-making authority regarding the content and priorities of the Product Backlog. Collaborates with the team and stakeholders.

Figure 5.9 Key points: Product owner[25]

Project Manager[26] holds authoritative and decision-making responsibilities for project management aspects, the Product Owner has authority over product-related decisions, with the potential reporting structure of the Product Owner to the Project Manager. **The Sprint Backlog** is usually managed by the development team and **PB/Product Backlog Items by PO.**

5.5 Definition of Done (DoD) versus Definition of Ready (DoR)

Table 5.1 DoD versus DoR

Aspect	Definition of Done	Definition of Ready
Purpose	Criteria indicating completion of a task	Criteria indicating readiness to begin a task
Timing	Applied at the end of a task or sprint	Applied at the beginning of a task or sprint
Completion Standards	Focuses on quality and completeness	Focuses on readiness factors like requirements clarity
Criteria	Clear, measurable, and agreed-upon	Clearly defined and understood by the team
Acceptance	Determines if work meets expectations	Ensures that work can be started with minimal issues
Accountability	Shared understanding among team members	Ensures tasks are well-defined before implementation
Role	Defines when work is ready for review	Defines when work is ready to be started by the team

5.6 Questions for Practice

Burn-Up Chart Scenario

Project Scope: Develop a new e-commerce website.

Burn-Down Chart Scenario

Sprint Backlog: Implement a new feature in a two-week sprint.

Table 5.2 Story point details

Day	Planned Work (Story Points)	Remaining Work (Story Points)
1	40	40
2	40	35
3	40	25
4	40	15
5	40	5
6	40	0

Based on Burn-Up Chart (Q) Types

- **Question:** What is the cumulative work completed after Iteration 3?
  Answer: 55 Story Points

Based on Burn-Down Chart (Q) Types

- **Question:** How much work is remaining on Day 4?
  Answer: 15 Story Points

These scenarios and answers provide a basic understanding of how to interpret Burn-Up and Burn-Down charts in a project context.

Based on "Sprint Backlog"

Story Points Completed are as follows:

- Sprint 1: 20 Story Points
- Sprint 2: 25 Story Points
- Sprint 3: 18 Story Points
- Sprint 4: 30 Story Points
- Sprint 5: 22 Story Points

Questions

1. **Question:** What is the average velocity over the five sprints?
   - **Answer:** Average Velocity = 23
2. **Question:** What is the total velocity over the five sprints?
   - **Answer:** Total Velocity = Sum of Story Points, Total Velocity = 115
3. **Question:** What is the velocity for Sprint 3?
   - **Answer:** Velocity for Sprint 3 = Story Points Completed in Sprint 3 = 18

Multiple Choice Questions

1. What is the primary purpose of a Burn-Down chart in Agile?
   a. To visualize the progress of completed work
   b. To track the remaining work over time
   c. To estimate the team's velocity
   d. To display project costs

2. In a Burn-Down chart, what does the "ideal line" represent?
   a. The actual progress made by the team
   b. The expected progress based on the original plan
   c. The cumulative work completed
   d. The total backlog items

3. What is the key advantage of using a Burn-Up chart over a Burn-Down chart?
   a. It provides a clearer view of work completed.
   b. It shows the remaining work more accurately.
   c. It includes scope changes during the project.
   d. It is easier to draw and interpret.

4. In a Burn-Up chart, what does the area between the actual line and the ideal line represent?
   a. Completed work
   b. Scope changes
   c. Work in progress
   d. Unplanned work

5. When does the Burn-Down chart hit zero in an ideal scenario?
   a. When all work is completed
   b. At the start of the project
   c. When half of the work is completed
   d. When the team velocity is high

6. What is the primary focus of a Burn-Up chart?
   a. Tracking remaining work
   b. Visualizing completed work
   c. Predicting future work
   d. Monitoring team velocity

7. In a Burn-Down chart, how is velocity calculated?
   a. By dividing total story points by the number of sprints
   b. By measuring the distance between the actual line and the ideal line
   c. By counting the number of completed tasks
   d. By summing the story points completed in each sprint

8. What does the vertical axis of a Burn-Down chart represent?
   a. Time
   b. Work remaining
   c. Completed work
   d. Sprint numbers

9. In Agile, what does a sudden rise in the Burn-Up chart indicate?
   a. Increased team velocity
   b. Scope creep or additional work
   c. Accelerated project timeline
   d. Efficient task completion

10. What information does the Burn-Up chart communicate about scope changes?
    a. It ignores scope changes.
    b. It explicitly shows scope changes.
    c. It merges scope changes with completed work.
    d. It delays the impact of scope changes.

Answers: 1. b, 2. b, 3. c, 4. a, 5. a, 6. b, 7. d, 8. b, 9. b, 10. c

Other Question Types

1. **Burn-Down Velocity Calculation:**
   - In Sprint 1, a team completes 20 story points. In Sprint 2, they complete 25 story points. If the total planned story points for the project are 150, calculate the Burn-Down velocity after Sprint 2.

2. **Burn-Up with Scope Change:**
   - A project starts with 100 planned story points. After Sprint 3, the scope increases by 20 story points. If the team completes 15, 18, and 22 story points in Sprints 1, 2, and 3, calculate the final Burn-Up chart's cumulative completed work.

3. **Velocity and Remaining Work:**
   - A team completes 30 story points in Sprint 1 and 25 story points in Sprint 2. If the remaining planned story points are 120, calculate the team's velocity and the estimated remaining work after Sprint 2.

4. **Burn-Down with Variable Sprint Length:**
   - In a project with three sprints, the team completes 25, 30, and 35 story points. If Sprint 1 is two weeks, Sprint 2 is three weeks, and Sprint 3 is one week, calculate the average velocity per week and the estimated total work after Sprint 3.

5. **Burn-Up with Cumulative Scope Change:**
   - A project starts with 80 planned story points, and there are cumulative scope changes of +10, –5, and +15 story points after each sprint. If the team completes 20, 18, and 22 story points in the first three sprints, calculate the cumulative completed work in the Burn-Up chart.

6. **Velocity and Remaining Work After Scope Change:**
   - A team completes 25 story points in Sprint 1. After Sprint 2, there is a scope change adding 10 story points. If the team completes 20 story points in Sprint 2, calculate the revised velocity and the estimated remaining work after the scope change.

7. **Burn-Down Projection:**
   - In a project with a total of 120 planned story points, the team completes 30 story points in Sprint 1. If the Burn-Down chart follows a linear trend, project the expected work completed after Sprint 3.

8. **Burn-Up with Variable Completion Rates:**
   - A team completes 20, 25, and 15 story points in three sprints. Considering a variable completion rate of 80 percent, 90 percent, and 70 percent, calculate the cumulative completed work in the Burn-Up chart after each sprint.

Answers

1. Burn-Down Velocity Calculation:
   - After Sprint 2, the team has completed $20 + 25 = 45$ story points.
   - The remaining planned story points: $150 - 45 = 105$.
   - Burn-Down velocity after Sprint 2: $45/2 = 22.5$ story points per sprint.

2. Burn-Up with Scope Change:
   - Cumulative completed work after Sprint 3: $15 + 18 + 22 + 20 = 75$ story points.
   - Final cumulative completed work with scope change: $75 + 20 = 95$ story points.

3. Velocity and Remaining Work:
   - Velocity after Sprint 2: $(30 + 25)/2 = 55/2 = 27.5$ story points per sprint.
   - Estimated remaining work after Sprint 2: $120 - 55 = 65$ story points.

4. Burn-Down with Variable Sprint Length:
   - Average velocity per week: $(25/2) + (30/3) + (35/1) = 12.5 + 10 + 35 = 57.5/6 = 9.58$ story points per week.
   - Estimated total work after Sprint 3: $25 + 30 + 35 = 90$ story points.

5. Burn-Up with Cumulative Scope Change:
   - Cumulative completed work after three sprints:
     $20 + 18 + 22 + 10 - 5 + 15 = 80$ story points.
6. Velocity and Remaining Work After Scope Change:
   - Revised velocity after scope change:
     $(25 + 20)/2 = 45/2 = 22.5$ story points per sprint.
   - Estimated remaining work after scope change: $120 - 45 = 75$ story points.
7. Burn-Down Projection:
   - Expected work completed after Sprint 3: $(30/1)*3 = 90$ story points.
8. Burn-Up with Variable Completion Rates:
   - Cumulative completed work after each sprint:
     ○ Sprint 1: $20*0.8 = 16$ story points
     ○ Sprint 2: $25*0.9 = 22.5$ story points
     ○ Sprint 3: $15*0.7 = 10.5$ story points

References

1. Larson, E. and C. Gray. 2021 *Project Management: The Managerial Process*. 8th ed. Boston: McGraw-Hill Education.
2. Phillips, J. 2018. *PMP Project Management Professional Study Guide*. 5th ed. Indianapolis: Sybex.
3. Reichel, C.W. 2006. *Earned Value Management Systems (EVMS): 'You Too Can Do Earned Value Management'*. Paper presented at PMI® Global Congress 2006—North America, Seattle, WA, Newtown Square, PA: Project Management Institute.
4. Sawle, W.S. 1991. "Crisis Project Management." *PM Network* 5, no. 1, pp. 25–29.
5. Levy, F.K., G.L. Thompson, and J.D. Wiest. n.d. "The ABCs of the Critical Path Method." *Harvard Business Review*.
6. Parviz, F.R and L. Ginger. n.d. *Project Estimating and Cost Management*.
7. Angelo, C. n.d. *Understanding Financial Risk Management*. 1st ed. Routledge Advanced Texts in Economics and Finance. Routledge.
8. Amy, G. n.d. "A Refresher on Net Present Value." *Harvard Business Review*.
9. Project Management Institute. 2017. "A Guide to the Project Management Body of Knowledge (PMBOK Guide)." 6th ed. Project Management Institute.
10. Project Management Institute. 2024. "PMP Certification Exam Outline." Project Management Institute. www.pmi.org/certifications/types/project-management-pmp (accessed February 15, 2024).
11. Robin, C. and S.K. Robert. n.d. "Measure Costs Right: Make the Right Decisions." *Harvard Business Review*.
12. Boris, G. and C.B. Katherine. n.d. "Case Study: When Two Leaders on the Senior Team Hate Each Other." *Harvard Business Review*.
13. Andrew, R. n.d. *PMP Exam Prep Simplified*.

14. Harvard Business School. *2023* "Leading Change at Harley-Davidson." *Harvard Business School Publishing.* https://store.hbr.org/case-studies/ (accessed 2023).

15. Juran, J.M. and M.A. Godfrey. 2020. *Juran's Quality Handbook: A Guide to Continuous Improvement.* 7th ed. McGraw-Hill Education.

16. International Organization for Standardization. 2015 *ISO 9000:2015 Quality management systems—Fundamentals and Vocabulary.* Geneva, Switzerland: ISO.

17. Thomas, P. 2003. *The Six Sigma handbook: A Complete Guide for Green Belts, Black Belts, and Managers at All Levels.* Rev. and expanded ed. New York: McGraw-Hill.

18. Womack, J.P. and T.J. Daniel . 1996. *Lean Thinking: Banish Waste and Create Wealth in Your Corporation.* Simon and Schuster.

19. Project Management Institute (PMI). 2023. www.pmi.org/ (accessed December 2023).

20. Project Management Institute (PMI). 2021. *Project Management Body of Knowledge (PMBOK Guide) - Seventh Edition.* Newtown Square, PA: PMI Institute.

21. Project Management Institute (PMI). 2008. *A Guide to the Project Management Body of Knowledge (PMBOK Guide).* 4th ed. PA, Pennsylvania, Newtown Square: PMI Institute.

22. Tuckman, B.W. 1965. "Developmental Sequence in Small Groups." *Psychological Bulletin* 63, no. 6, pp. 384399.

23. Patty, M. n.d. "Situational Leadership Model (Hersey and Blanchard)."

24. Thomas, K.W. and R.H. Kilmann. 1996. *Conflict Mode Instrument: User's Guide.* CPP, Inc.

25. Scrum Alliance. November 2020. "The Scrum Guide." Scrum Alliance. www.scrumalliance.org/scrum-guide

26. PMI. 2017. "Agile Practice Guide." Project Management Institute.

About the Author

Rupal Jain is a distinguished figure in the field of semiconductor chip manufacturing, with extensive expertise in engineering, program management, and strategic alignment. Throughout her career, she has spearheaded projects encompassing the entire chip development lifecycle—from design conception and quality management to global delivery across regions like the United States, Taiwan, Singapore, Italy, Malaysia, China, and India. Her profound knowledge is recognized by prestigious certifications like PMP, CSM, and Lean Six Sigma Black Belt. Rupal holds a master's degree in Electrical and Electronics Engineering, earned through a joint program between NTU Singapore and TUM Germany.

Beyond her technical prowess, Rupal's innovative contributions have garnered international acclaim. She is a frequent contributor to esteemed publications, serves on prestigious juries, and holds nominated memberships in industry organizations. Notably, her work has been recognized with coveted awards and patents, further solidifying her position as a leader in the field. Her other authored pieces, *Semiconductor Essentials: A Leader's Express Reference to Electronics Concepts* and *Advancements in AI and IoT for Chip Manufacturing and Defect Prevention*, promise to share her valuable insights with the next generation of leaders and engineers.

Index

www.ingramcontent.com/pod-product-compliance
Lightning Source LLC
Chambersburg PA
CBHW061211220326
41599CB00025B/4604